Anonymous

Testimony in the Contested Election

of Brooke vs. Widdicombe, of Prince George's County, Md.

Anonymous

Testimony in the Contested Election
of Brooke vs. Widdicombe, of Prince George's County, Md.

ISBN/EAN: 9783337170622

Printed in Europe, USA, Canada, Australia, Japan

Cover: Foto ©Suzi / pixelio.de

More available books at **www.hansebooks.com**

[Document K.]

BY THE HOUSE OF DELEGATES,

JANUARY 30TH, 1874.

Read and 500 copies ordered to be printed.

By order,

MILTON Y. KIDD,

Chief Clerk.

TESTIMONY

IN THE

CONTESTED ELECTION

OF

BROOKE VS. WIDDICOMBE,

OF

PRINCE GEORGE'S COUNTY, MD.

ANNAPOLIS:

S. S. MILLS & L. F. COLTON, PRINTERS TO THE HOUSE OF DELEGATES.

1874.

DEPOSITIONS.

HENRY BROOKE AGAINST ROBERT S. WIDDICOMBE,

BEFORE THE

HOUSE OF DELEGATES OF THE STATE OF MARYLAND.

Depositions taken before me, James Harris, a Justice of the Peace of the State of Maryland, in and for Prince George's County:

Be it remembered, and I hereby certify, that Henry Brooke above named filed with me, a Justice of the Peace, as aforesaid, a notice and return marked Contestant's Exhibit A., which I herewith return as a part of this Record, *vide* Exhibit "A."

And be it further remembered, that said Henry Brooke applied to me, James Harris, a Justice as aforesaid, to take testimony in the above entitled case, and I thereupon issued the following notices, to wit:—(*vide* notices marked Exhibits B. and C.)—which said notices, with returns, affidavit of service and certificate endorsed thereon, I herewith return as part of this record, marked Exhibit B. and C.

[L. S.]   JAMES HARRIS,

Justice of the Peace of the State of Maryland in and for Prince George's County.

EXHIBIT "A."

To ROBERT S. WIDDICOMBE, ESQ.:

Sir—Notice is hereby given that it is my intention to contest your election for the Clerkship of the Circuit Court for Prince George's County, Maryland. I shall proceed to take testimony at such time and place as shall hereafter be designated and agreed upon by James Harris, a Justice of the Peace of the State of Maryland in and for Prince George's County.

HENRY BROOKE.

Dated this 1st day of December, 1873.

UPPER MARLBORO', PRINCE GEORGE'S COUNTY, MD.,
December 3, 1873.

I hereby certify that I did, on the 2d day of December, 1873, serve upon Robert S. Widdicombe a copy of the foregoing and annexed notice by leaving the same at his usual residence near Lanham's Postoffice, Prince George's County, Maryland, and that the said Robert S. Widdicombe was absent at the time, but has this day acknowledged to me that he received said notice.

H. WALLIS, *Sheriff.*

Filed with me, this 26th day of January, 1874.

[L. S.]   JAMES HARRIS,
Justice of the Peace.

EXHIBIT "B."

To ROBERT S. WIDDICOMBE:

Sir—You are hereby notified that in accordance with Section 52, of Article 35, of the Code of Public General Laws of Maryland, as amended by the Act of 1865, chapter 143, relating to contested elections, Henry Brooke, who is contesting your election as Clerk of the Circuit Court for Prince George's County, under the election held on the 4th day of November, in the year 1873, in said county, has applied to the undersigned, a Justice of the Peace of the State of Maryland, in and for Prince George's County aforesaid, for a notice under my hand and seal, to be directed to you, notifying you that he will examine before me the persons as witnesses, who are hereinafter named, to wit:

Charles Clagett, William B. Hill, Rector Pumphrey, James G. Wedding, Charles H. Gill, Thomas J. Turner, Frederick Sasscer, Joseph K. Roberts, Jr., John W. Medley, William A. Jarboe, Sr., George W. Richardson, John H. Bartley, Basil Brown, Thomas Clagett, Charles C. Hill, John W. Belt

(Oak Grove), John Garmhaw, Captain B. F. Gwynn, Jeremiah Berry, Richard Woolton, Samuel Peach, Richard Peach, James Mullikin, William Edelen, G. L. Baldwin, Wm. B. Bowie, James L. Brashears, Washington Johnston, Barney West, James H. Ritchie, Jeremiah Coffen, Thos. R. Brooks, John S. Ritchie, Lewis R. Sewall, Judson F. Richardson, Singleton Wehter, Nathan Masters, Nicholas Brookes, Dr. P. H. Heiskill, John A. Fraser, John W. Webster, John J. R. Steed, James A. Gregory, James W. Richards, George E. Orme.

By the above witnesses he expects to prove—

First. That said election was not conducted in the manner designated by the Constitution and laws of Maryland.

Second. That owing to intimidation legally qualified voters were prevented from voting at said election.

Third. That legally qualified voters were prevented from voting at said election by other causes.

Fourth. That minors were allowed to vote at said election.

Fifth. That unpardoned convicts were permitted to vote at said election.

Sixth. That non-residents of said State and county were permitted to vote at said election.

Seventh. That the returns of said election were not made out, returned, and certified according to the laws of this State.

Eighth. That through the unlawful interference of candidates and others at said election, legally qualified voters were deceived and prevented from voting for him the said contestant.

And you are further notified that the said contestant shall offer in evidence certified copies and extracts from the poll and registration books of the respective districts of said county.

You are therefore hereby notified to attend in person, or by attorney, at the Court House, in the town of Upper Marlborough, on Monday, the 22d day of December, 1873, at 10 o'clock A. M., to cross-examine witnesses, and do such other matters in the premises as you desire.

And you are further notified that if such testimony cannot all be taken on the day named, the taking of the same will be continued from day to day until the same is completed.

Given under my hand and seal this 9th day of December, 1873.

[L. s.]   JAMES HARRIS,
                                Justice of the Peace.

1873, December 10, I hereby certify that I this day served the notice above upon Robert S. Widdicombe, by leaving a copy of the same with his wife, at his usual residence, near Lanham's Postoffice, Prince George's County, Maryland, and and that I subsequently met the said Robert S. Widdicombe in Washington City, D. C., and notified him of the same on the same day.

                                H. WALLIS, *Sheriff.*

EXHIBIT "C."

To ROBERT S. WIDDICOMBE:

Sir—You are hereby notified, that in accordance with Section 52 of Art. 35 of the Code of Public General Laws of Maryland, as amended by the Act of 1865, chapter 143, relating to contested elections, Henry Brooke, who is contesting your election as Clerk of the Circuit Court for Prince George's County, under the election held on the fourth day of November, in the year 1873, in said County, has applied to the undersigned, a Justice of the Peace of the State of Maryland, in and for Prince George's County aforesaid, for a notice under my hand and seal, to be directed to you, notifying you that he will examine before me the persons as witnesses who are hereinafter named, to wit:

A. T. Brooke, John M. Roberts, L. O. Hodges, James H. Ritchie, Upton Hodges, John W. Belt, George W. Wilson, Jr., William H. Harper, Staley N. Magruder, Richard H. Sasscer, John B. Brooke, Robert Clarke, J. R. H. Deakins, Benjamin F. Guy, Edward Ryan, James Shreeve, Thomas J. Frazier, John L. Gray, John H. S. Sasscer, Patrick Fleming, John Price, William J. Hill, Joseph L. Jarboe, C. C. Magruder, Jr., William A. Jarboe, Jr., Robert V. Pumphrey, Enos J. Pumphrey, Robert H. Pumphrey.

By the above witnesses he expects to prove—

First. That the said election was not conducted in the manner designated by the Constitution and Laws of Maryland.

Second. That owing to intimidation, legally qualified voters were prevented from voting at said election.

Third. That legally qualified voters were prevented from voting at said election by other causes.

Fourth. That minors were allowed to vote at said election.

Fifth. That unpardoned convicts were permitted to vote at said election.

Sixth. That non-residents of said County and State were permitted to vote at said election.

Seventh. That the returns of said election were not made out, returned and certified according to the laws of the State.

Eighth. That through the unlawful interference of candidates and others at said election, legally qualified voters were deceived and prevented from voting for him, the said contestant.

And you are further notified that the said contestant shall offer in evidence certified copies and extracts from the poll and registration books of the respective districts of said County.

You are therefore hereby notified to attend in person or by attorney at the Court House in the Town of Upper Marlborough, on the fifth day of January, 1874, at 10 o'clock, A. M., to cross-examine witnesses and do such other matters in the premises as you desire.

And you are further notified that if such testimony cannot all be taken on the day named, the taking of the same will be continued from day to day until the same is completed.

Given under my hand and seal this twenty-fourth day of January, 1874.

[L. S.]   JAMES HARRIS, J. P.

STATE OF MARYLAND, PRINCE GEORGE'S COUNTY, SCT:

I HEREBY CERTIFY, That on this 29th day of December, Anno Domini, 1873, personally appeared John W. Medley, before me, the subscriber, a Justice of the Peace of said State, in and for said County, and made oath on the Holy Evangely of Almighty God that he did serve the within notice upon George C. Merrick, attorney for Robert S. Widdicombe, on the 24th day of December, A. D., 1873, and delivered him in writing a copy of the same on the said day.

JAMES H. RITCHIE, J. P.

STATE OF MARYLAND, PRINCE GEORGE'S COUNTY, SCT:

I HEREBY CERTIFY, That James H. Ritchie, Esq:, before whom the annexed affidavit was made, and who has thereto subscribed his name, was, at the time of so doing, a Justice of the Peace of the State of Maryland, in and for the County of Prince George's, duly commissioned and sworn.

In Testimony Whereof, I hereto set my hand and affix the seal of the Circuit Court for Prince George's County, this 30th day of December, Anno Domini, 1873.

[L.S.]   HENRY BROOKE,
Clerk of the Circuit Court for Prince George's County.

UPPER MARLBOROUGH, PRINCE GEORGE'S CO., MD., }
December 22d, 1873. }

In pursuance of the aforegoing notice, I attended at the time and place therein designated, and having appointed Richard E. Brandt as clerk, and administered to him an oath to fairly write down and transcribe the depositions to be taken by me, did proceed then and there to take the following testimony, to wit:

DEPOSITION No. 1.

WM. B. BOWIE, being duly sworn and examined, deposed and said as follows, to-wit:

State your name, age, occupation, and residence, and in what election district you voted on the 4th of November, 1873, the day of election?

My name is Wm. B. Bowie, aged 60; occupation, farmer; residence, Marlborough district, Prince George's County. I voted in the Third Election District of Prince George's County.

2d Question.—Do you know of any non-residents of the county or State who voted with the Republican party at the election held on the 4th November, 1873, and how long has each of said parties removed from said county, and where do they now reside?

Witness does not know how any one voted, except himself and sons. He knows of men living out of the State who voted at said election, but I, as Register, did not erase their names. Mr. Eugene Brooke, one of said parties, removed from the county, he thinks, nearly three years; Mr. Albert Brooke removed from the county, I think, nearly two years; George Bowling, I think, has been away nearly two years. All of them reside in Washington City.

3d Question.—Do you know of any interference by candidates or other parties with any voter or voters of said election?

I don't know of any interference by candidates, but I did see interfering by other parties with a negro man, named Alex. Gross; they were hauling and pulling in such a manner that he went to his rescue, not knowing how he wished to vote, when he said that he wanted to vote for Messrs. Clark and Brooke. I came to the Court House door with him and remained there with him, I suppose, about half an hour, and could not get in, and he left and went away without voting.

4th Question.—Was or was not said election, at said polls, fairly conducted in your opinion; if not, state your reasons for such opinion?

It may have been, but in my opinion it was not. Because the polls were obstructed and voters could not get in. I saw no violence. The polls were obstructed by the colored voters because they were very numerous.

5th Question.—Did you or not see any colored men or speakers from Washington City, or non-resident of the county, at or near the polls on that day attempting to intimidate the colored voters?

I saw a colored man, I think named Buttler, not a voter of this county, to my knowledge, speaking in the Court House yard, trying to influence votes for the Republican party.

Cross-examined by Mr. Merrick, attorney for Mr. Widdicombe:

1st Question.—State how you know that Eugene Brooke, Albert Brooke and George Bowling had been residing out of the county more than two years, as stated in your examination-in-chief, and when you first learned that fact?

I heard it from their own lips that they were living there. I have known for twelve months that all of the parties have resided in Washington City.

2d Question.—State, if you please, why, if you knew for twelve months that the parties were non-residents of the county and State, you did not as Register erase their names from the Registration books of this county?

The best reason in the world; before the last days of revision, I received the United States election laws through the postoffice, and that was the cause of my not erasing many names, but I don't say that I would have erased their names if I had not received them. Receiving those laws had the effect of intimidating and making me very cautious how I acted.

3d Question.—Did you as a sworn Officer of Registration allow the names of any person or persons to remain upon your list of registered and qualified voters who you knew of, or believed, were not entitled to vote on the 4th of November, 1873?

I answer no, and if I had known of any parties positively whose names were upon that list, and not entitled to be there, I would have erased them if I had been put in jail afterwards. Mr. Suit told me about the United States laws, and that they were superior to the State laws, and that if we did not carry it out that we would be prosecuted, and that was the cause of my not correcting the books as closely as I would have done. I remarked to Mr. Suit that I would discharge my duty, under the State law; I think, but I am not positive, that Mr. Suit told me that he sent me the United States laws.

4th Question.—You have stated in your examination-in-chief that one Alen Gross was interfered with by certain parties on the day of the election and that you went up with him to vote. State whether you know of any interference with the said Alen Gross after you went with him to the Court House for the purpose of voting, and whether or not he was at liberty to remain as long as he pleased and go where he chose.

I don't know of any interference after that.

5th Question.—State whether or not, when you and Mr. Widdicombe went where the parties were pulling and hauling Gross, he was allowed to go with you, as you desired, to the Court House for the purpose of voting.

There was no interference; he was allowed to go with me.

6th Question.—You state in your examination-in-chief that the polls were obstructed by colored voters. State whether or not the parties were not there for the purpose of voting, and if the obstruction was not in consequence of the large numbers having to wait for their opportunity to vote?

Yes.

Re-examined by Mr. Roberts, attorney for Mr. Brooke:

Was there not a band of music from Washington, and non-residents of the County and State helping to influence the vote and obstruct the polls.

There was music, but I do not know where it came from. There were non-residents in the crowd and the crowd did obstruct the polls. I don't think the music obstructed the polls.

Cross-examined by Mr. Merrick:

State, if you please, how long the music remained in the vicinity of the polls, and how long the voters or any crowd obstructed the polls, and if there was not a period of several hours before the closing of the polls when there was no crowd of voters or other persons in or about the voting place obstructing the polls?

I did not remain all day, but saw a crowd as long as I remained. I left about three o'clock.

W. B. BOWIE.

Test: JAMES HARRIS.

DEPOSITION No. 2.

MR. RESTOR PUMPHREY being next duly sworn and examined, deposed as follows:

State your name, age, occupation, residence and in what election district did you vote on the 4th November, 1873, and whether you were one of the Judges of the election?

My name is Restor Pumphrey, aged 60, farmer, Marlborough District, Prince George's County. I voted in the Third Election District on the 4th November, 1873, and was one of the Judges of the election on that day.

2d Question.—Do you know of any non-residents of the County or State who voted with the Republican party on the 4th November, 1873, at the election polls of said district? How long since each of said parties removed from the county and where they now reside?

I do not know of any non-residents that voted with the Republican party.

3d Question.—Do you know whether Eugene Brooke voted at said polls on said day of election, and, if so, what ticket he voted?

I know that Mr. Eugene Brooke voted ; he voted an opened Republican ticket.

4th Question.—Do you or not know of any obstruction of voters at the polls on the said day of election, and whether the officers of the law on that day were able to prevent such obstruction ?

Complaint was made to me, as Judge of Election, in relation to obstruction at the front door of the Court House. I called and ordered Mr. Wedding, constable, to go and clear the way so that all legal voters might have free access to the polls. Complaints being made to me afterwards, I ordered him, and he stated that he could not clear the obstruction out of the way.

5th Question.—Did you see any interference by candidates or other parties with voters at the polls on that day ?

Mr. Richard Sansbury seized a colored man in the collar that was approaching the polls to vote, and I ordered him to let the man go ; he did so after ordered. I would further state that Mr. John W. Duvall, with boisterous language and curses, made some noise and disturbance close to the polls, but it soon subsided.

Cross-examined by Mr. Merrick :

1st Question.—You have stated that Mr. Eugene Brooke voted an open Republican ticket. State whether you examined that ticket and whether or not some of the printed names were not scratched from said ticket?

I examined no man's ticket. The heading was a Republican ticket. I can't say whether it was scratched or not. I saw no scratch on it.

2d Question.—State who made complaint to you about the obstruction at the front door, and whether such obstruction was from violence or in consequence of the crowd seeking for opportunity to vote, and whether persons did not, that day, come in through both the front and rear door of the Court House for the purpose of voting, and whether, after the crowd had voted in the morning, there were not several hours in the afternoon that scarcely any persons voted at all, Mr. Charles C. Hill, Charles Clagett, Mr. Joseph K. Roberts, Wm. B. Hill and others?

It was stated to me that the door was obstructed, that none

but the Republican party could vote. It was stated to me that the obstruction was violence. The impression left on my mind is, that it was a promiscuous crowd of parties from Washington and voters, who prevented any one from voting the Democratic ticket. Can't say how many feet the crowd was from the polls. My information in this matter was received from others. I will state that after Mr. Wedding had reported that he could not clear the obstruction to the polls, for one hour and a half or two hours after the polls were opened, then I ordered and directed that the rear door, next to the Clerk's office, should be kept by some one, and admit five persons to enter and approach the polls to vote and return the same way; and also the same number should be admitted in at the front door; that privilege extended to the balance of the day. I was exceedingly busy receiving votes until a very late hour in the day.

3d Question.—You have stated that Mr. Duvall created some noise and disturbance near the polls by using boisterous language and cursing. State whether this disturbance prevented any voter from casting his ballot during that day?

It was a prevention at the time, and at my request it was stopped; and does not know whether it prevented any person from voting or not.

4th Question.—State, if you please, if there was not ample opportunity and time during that day for any one to vote who wished to do so and choose to remain until the close of the polls?

I have no practical knowledge of the fact of there not being time or opportunity to have voted in the space of time between the opening of the polls and the close of the same.

RECTOR PUMPHREY.

Test: JAMES HARRIS.

DEPOSITION No. 3.

MR. GEORGE E. ORME, being duly sworn, deposed as follows:

1st Question.—State your name, age, occupation, residence, and in what election district you voted on the 4th November, 1873.

My name is George E. Orme; age, 48; occupation, farmer;

residence, in Aquasco District, and voted in the Eighth Election District of Prince George's County.

2d Question.—Do you know of any person or persons who were prevented from voting as he or they desired on the said day of election? State fully all you know about it.

On the morning of the election, when I went out of the door about daybreak, Sam Hall, colored, was standing at the door. I asked him what he wanted. He said he wanted to vote the Democratic ticket; that he was afraid the black people would beat him if I did not go up there with him. I told him that I would go up there with him and that no one should hurt him. About the time I thought the polls were opened, I went with him up to Horse Head, the place of election. When I got there the polls were not opened, and I told Sam that he could go around there where they were fixing breakfast and stay until the polls were opened. He went to the kitchen or quarter; the polls were opened; the crowd was voting: I went to get my breakfast about fifty yards from the polls. I stayed a few minutes and came back; somebody told me that they were voting Sam Hall around there and he did not want to vote. I went into the room of the Judges of the election and I heard Sam Hall say that is not my name. "My name is not Samuel R. Hall, certain." One of the Judges of the election had his ticket in his hand when I got there. I told Sam to come around where I was. He said, "that is not my name, and I don't want to vote by that name." The Judges were then talking, whether they should receive his vote or not. I said, Sam, do you want to vote that ticket Mr. Rowlins, one of the Judges, has in his hand, or this which I have, which was a Democratic ticket. He said, if I have got to vote by that name, I want to vote this ticket, being the one which I handed, a Democratic ticket. Somebody said he could not vote twice, and Mr. Rowlins put the ticket he had in the box. I told Mr. Rowlins that he ought to give the ticket back. Sam Hall said he did not vote the ticket he wanted to vote.

Cross-examined by Mr. Merrick:

1st Question.—How long have you known Sam Hall?

I have known him three or four years.

2d Question.—Does he live upon your land?

He hired himself to a Mr. Tennyson and rented a house from me for his wife and children, and that was his house when he was not at Mr. Tennyson's, but the house burned down just a short time before the election.

3d Question.—Where did his family go after the house was burned, and had Samuel Hall and yourself ever any conversation, prior to the election, as to how he, Sam, would vote?

His family went to her brother's. I had not seen him for six months prior to the election, nor never said a word to him about voting until the day of the election. He was in my debt at the time of the election.

4th Question.—When did you give him a Democratic ticket?

I gave it to him when the dispute was going on about his voting and when Mr. Rowlins was holding the other ticket in his hand.

G. E. ORME.

Test: JAMES HARRIS.

DEPOSITION No. 4.

JAMES H. GREGORY, being duly sworn, deposes and says:

1st Question.—State your name, age, occupation, residence and your place of voting on the 4th November, 1873?

My name is James A. Gregory, age 52, merchant, Prince George's County, the Fifth Election District of said County.

2d. Question.—Do you know of any intimidation used to prevent persons from voting Democratic tickets at the election held on the 4th of November, 1873?

Yes, I saw several instances; one was: some parties went with me to the election; they were headed off from the window where the tickets were voted. They said they could not get there to vote, and were threatened that if they voted a Democratic ticket they would be killed. After some time I succeeded in getting them out of the crowd, or they followed me out. They then went in the back way, as they were prevented from getting to the window where the ballots were received, having been pulled and hauled about so as to prevent them. This was done on account of their wanting to vote the Democratic ticket, by voters of the opposite party, set on by men living in Washington, who were present there at the polls, aiding in crowding off the voters that were not voting their way.

3d Question.—Do you know of any person or persons prevented from voting a Democratic ticket by intimidation that day?

John Hawkins and Badley Queen said that they were compelled to vote the Republican ticket that day, or not vote at all. The colored men from Washington on several occasions crowded off voters, and threatened to beat those that were going to vote the Democratic ticket.

Cross-examined by Mr. Merrick, counsel for Mr. Widdicombe:

1st Question.—Are the persons referred to in your testimony the only ones who were prevented from voting that day?

They are the only ones he knows of positively.

2d Question.—Did the parties whom you say went in the back way succeed in voting their sentiments?

They did vote the way they wanted, and were threatened to be killed when they came out. Does not know who made the threat; it came from the crowd; I heard it. Does not know whether John Hawkins and Bradly Queen voted or not.

3d Question.—Was there or not ample opportunity and time between the opening and closing of the polls for every one wishing to vote to do so?

Yes. There was plenty of time for all to vote, if those that after voting had not stood at the window and obstructed it so as to prevent others from getting to the window.

4th Question.—State, if you please, if you know of any persons voting the Republican ticket, who were carried in and voted by the back way, and whether you experienced any difficulty or obstruction in carrying in the parties whom you carried in?

There were several persons who voted the Republican ticket who came in the back way. I had a good deal of trouble in getting in the back way, the way being blocked up by the crowd.

5th Question.—Did any one attempt to prevent you from taking these persons in the back way? If so, how did they attempt to prevent you?

They did attempt, and did it by blocking up the gate and

by holding on to the men, and threatening what they would do with them, and to beat them when they came out. I could not tell who the parties were. I know that one of the parties who was in the crowd was from Washington.

6th Question.—Had not the Democrats access to this back way by which voters came in and voted?

No more than the other party had.

7th Question.—Was there as much obstruction the back way as there was the front way?

There was not.

8th Question.—Was not voting going on all the time the crowd was round about the window, and was not the crowd principally composed of persons who were there for the purpose of voting?

Voting was not going on all the time the crowd was around the window. Sometimes it was considerable time when a voter could not get up to the window, caused by a crowd being around the window, composed partly by persons from Washington. There were several strangers there, but can't say how many.

9th Question.—State how long at any one time, to your own knowledge, it was impossible for one desiring to vote to get to the window where voting took place, and whether the crowd around and about the voting place was not composed of members of both parties, and if there was any time, and if so, how long, when voters could not get in the back way?

I could not tell the exact time, as I did not notice. Did not expect to be called upon in reference to it. Knew some parties that went off and sat down to wait. The crowd around the window was not composed of persons of both parties.

10th Question.—State whether the crowd about the window was there for the purpose of voting or preventing others from voting ; and if there was any period of the day when the witness would have been in danger of violence to his person by quietly attempting to voting his sentiments, and if the obstruction at the polls, such as he speaks of, was different or greater than at the last one or two elections prior to this?

It must have been to prevent voting, as he did not see any voting going on when the crowd was about the window. If I had been of the same color, perhaps, but I did not appre-

2

hend any. I never saw an election conducted as this was, except once during the war, when the soldiers obstructed the polls; this time the polls having been obstructed by parties living out of the State.

11*th Question.*—You have said in your examination-in-chief, that parties were obstructed in attempting to vote a Democratic ticket. Now state if there was any blood shed, and if any one was injured in their person while said voting was going on, in consequence of voting or wishing to vote the Democratic ticket?

I saw a man that had been struck who had his face badly mashed, but I did not see the lick struck. I understood that he was struck for voting the Democratic ticket. I know that he always voted a Democratic ticket.

Re-examined:

1*st Question.*—If the election had been conducted in a proper and legal manner, could not the ballots have been deposited by the voters in one-half the time that was consumed?

Yes, sir.

J. A. GREGORY.

Test: JAMES HARRIS, J. P.

CHARLES CLAGETT, being duly sworn, deposes and says:

1*st Question.*—State your name, age, occupation, residence, and in what election district you voted on the 4th of November, 1873?

My name is Charles Clagett; age, 52 years; occupation, farmer; residence, in Marlboro' district, Prince George's county, and voted in the Third Election District of said county.

2*d Question.*—Do you know or not whether Eugene Brooke, Albert Brooke and George Bowling resided in Prince George's County on the day of election, and if not, how long since they were residents of said county and State, and where they then resided?

Eugene Brooke, Albert Brooke and George Bowling did not reside in Prince George's County on the day of election. I do not know exactly, but can't have been for two years. They have resided and did reside on the day of election in Washington City, to the best of my knowledge and belief.

3*d Question.*—Do you know of any interference by any candidate or other party with any voter or voters at said election?

Yes. Mr. Widdicombe remained in the Court House, around the polls, about three-fourths of the day, taking tickets from voters, tearing them up or throwing them on the ground and giving them others in their place.

4th Question.—State whether you saw or heard of any intimidation used at or about said polls in order to control votes?

Yes. There was a crowd of negroes gathered around the front door of the Court House for, perhaps, about twenty feet square, composed of negroes who were disorderly, boisterous and threatening. The crowd around the door was evidently then for the purpose of intimidation. Whilst the crowd was there a negro was speaking, and thereby exciting and urging the crowd to keep up this disorder.

5th Question.—Was or was not the said election, in your opinion, fairly conducted; and if not, state your reasons for such opinion?

It was not fairly conducted, because the crowd, in my opinion, was in a measure to intimidate voters.

6th Question.—Was or was not free access to the polls prevented by a disorderly crowd, composed of non-residents and others, attempting to control and influence votes?

Yes. It continued so from the time I got there up to one or two o'clock.

7th Question.—Do you know of any other matter or thing that would be of any other advantage to the contestant?

I saw Mr. Flint, one of the Judges of the Election, when a colored man came up to cast his ballot, lay it down on the table where the box was to be put in the box, when he, the said Flint, picked up another, and asked him to vote it.

8th Question.—Was Mr. Flint a Republican or Democrat?

He is a Republican.

Cross-examined by Mr. Merrick:

1st Question.—You have stated that Eugene Brooke, Albert Brooke and George Bowling had not been residents of Prince George's County for two years. Please state how you know this, and whether you know of either of the parties ever having voted out side of Prince George's County in the last two years?

I have seen them in Washington frequently, and Mr. Eugene Brooke has been keeping store there; his wife and family

reside there.   I have seen Albert Brooke in Washington and
living with his mother.   I have seen Bowling there frequently ;
his family reside there and he told me so.

2d Question.—Have not the three above-named parties,
Eugene Brooke, Albert Brooke and George Bowling, before
they went to Washington, been qualified voters in Prince
George's County and removed from here to Washington, and
state further if you know whether it is their purpose to remain
permanently in Washington City or return again to this
County ?

When they were living here I think they were qualified voters.   I do not know whether they intend to remain permanently in Washington or return again.

3d Question.—You state Mr. Widdicombe remained three-
fourths of the day, at least, in the Court House and around
the polls, taking tickets from voters, tearing some up and
throwing others on the ground and giving them others in
their places.   State, if you please, any one particular case you
can remember ?

I saw him take not less than a dozen tickets from parties
and maybe twenty-five ; one in particular, I remember, a man
in my employ, named Barney ——.

4th Question.—State further, if you are positive, if you saw
Mr. Widdicombe tear up any tickets which you saw him get
from voters, whether he obtained said tickets by violence or
not, and whether said parties did not go away of their own
will from where Mr. Widdicombe was, without any violence or
force, after he gave the other tickets ?

I saw him tear up some ; I did not see any violence used by
Mr. Widdicombe in the obtention of said tickets.   I saw no
violence used by Mr. Widdicombe.   But my impression is
that the parties thought they were obliged to show their
tickets and vote the ones that he gave them.

5th Question.—Was Mr. Widdicombe the only one witness
you saw take tickets from voters and give others in their stead,
and did not the witness see Democratic candidates take tickets
from voters and give them others in their stead?   Does not
witness know of such having been done by Democratic candidates at this election, and if it is not a usual and ordinary
custom for candidates and others at elections held in this

county, quietly and without force to get the tickets from persons of opposite political views and induce them to vote your way whenever you can?

Mr. Widdicombe was the only one I saw inside the Court House and around the polls take tickets from voters, and I don't think I saw any one outside. I did not see Democratic candidates take tickets from voters. I never knew it to be done inside of the Court House by Democratic candidates. I know that the custom is to influence them, but have never seen any one take tickets from them inside of the Court House.

6th Question.—You have stated that there was a crowd near the Court House, there, in your opinion, for intimidating voters, and a negro man speaking, thereby urging the crowd to disorder. State, if you please, whether you heard the colored speaker referred to use any language advising the crowd to disorder; if there was not ample time between the opening and closing the polls for every one wishing to vote to do so?

I can't give his language, but the whole speech was calculated and designed for this purpose. A part of the day, up to about one o'clock, it was with great difficulty for a Democrat to get into the Court House to vote, and the latter part of the day they had ample opportunity.

7th Question.—You say the election was not fairly conducted because, in your opinion, the crowd was there to intimidate voters. State, if you know of any persons who were intimidated and thereby prevented from voting; if yes, give their names.

· I do not know of any one who was prevented by intimidation, but my opinion is that persons were prevented from voting the Democratic ticket, being under the impression that they had to show their tickets, and the tickets that were given them they had to vote.

8th Question.—You state that access to the polls was obstructed until about one o'clock by non-residents and others. State, if you please, whether voting was not going on during all the day, from nine until six o'clock, through the front door of the Court House, and from the time the Judge directed the back door to be opened, voting was not going on through both the front and the rear doors of the Court House?

Yes, I think it was going on slowly, and parties after voting, instead of leaving, went back in the crowd around the door, for the purpose of intimidation, in my opinion.

9th Question.—State whether the voter to whom you saw Mr. Flint hand a ticket and asked to vote it, voted the ticket he brought in to vote or the one handed him by Mr. Flint?

I think he voted the ticket he brought in, and not the one handed him by Mr. Flint.

Re-examined by Mr. Roberts:

1st. Question.—Do you or not know Minor Pooles (colored)? If yea, when did he leave this county, and where did he go to live?

I know Minor Pooles; he left here about nearly two years ago and removed to Washington, where he resided ever since with his family.

Cross-examined by Mr. Merrick:

1st Question.—How do you know that Minor Pooles, whom you say removed to Washington two years ago, how do you know that he has resided there ever since, and do you know whether his purpose in moving was to remain permanently away, and whether or not you know of his having voted in this county?

I have seen him several times, and he said he was living there. I don't know what he intends to do, but he is living there. I do not know of his voting anywhere but in this county.

CHAS. CLAGGETT.

Test: JAMES HARRIS.

JOHN A. FRASER, being duly sworn, deposed as follows:

1st Question.—State your name, age, occupation, and residence, and in what district you voted on the 4th November, 1873.

My name is John A. Fraser; age, 42; occupation, farmer; voted in Surratt, Ninth Election District, Prince George's County, on the 4th November, 1873.

2d Question.—Do you or not know of any person or persons who voted in the Ninth Election District, on the day of election, a Republican ticket, who were non-residents of the County or State, or otherwise disqualified to vote?

I know of two parties, namely: John McNally, who told

me he was going to vote the whole of the Republican, with the exception of Mr. Underwood for Sheriff, and Mr. Piles for Commissioner; he is a resident of Washington City, and has been for two or three years. The other non-resident is Francis Allen; resided a portion of the time in New Jersey, and the other part of the time in Washington City; has been a non-resident of this State for about two years, so far as I recollect of at this time. George Locker, an unpardoned convict, also voted in said district; on said day he voted with the Republican party; I also saw two men registered on the day of election, who voted the Republican ticket; also, James Young, who had recently removed from Spalding's District, voted on said day; voted the Republican ticket, to the best of my knowledge and belief.

Cross-examined by Mr. Merrick:

1st Question.—You say that John McNally voted the Republican ticket, except for Sheriff and one Commissioner. How do you know that he voted, and in the manner you stated?

He told me before the election that he was going to vote that way, and has told me since the election that he had voted that way.

2d Question.—State, if you please, how you know that he is a non-resident, and if you know that his removal from the county is permanent or not.

Three or four years ago he lived within a half mile of my outside line; he removed from thence to Spalding's District, and from thence to Washington; I can't say whether his removal is permanent or not, but he thinks it is.

3d Question.—Do you know whether said McNally has ever voted out of Prince George's County; also, whether Francis Allen has ever voted out of Prince George's County since his removal from the county, and if you know that the said Francis Allen has permanently removed from the county?

I don't know whether either of the above has ever voted out of the county; I know that he has sold his real estate in the county, and has no monied interest in the county.

4th Question.—How do you know that the said Francis Allen voted the Republican ticket?

I saw Mr. Robey, the Republican candidate, give him a ticket; I followed him to the window and asked him to take on some of our candidates; he told me he could not do it.

5th Question.—State, if you please, how you know that George Locker voted the Republican ticket, and also how you know that he is an unpardoned convict, and if you know for what crime he was convicted.

He was with the crowd of Republicans, went up with them, and has since said in my hearing that he had deceived Mr. Brooke, George M. Wilson, and others ; as far as being an unpardoned convict, he was convicted of larceny, and as Deputy Sheriff, I assisted in carrying him to the penitentiary, and that he did not register or vote when the negroes were first enfranchised, and that is my reason for thinking that he is an unpardoned convict.

6th Question.—State how you know that James Young voted the Republican ticket, and also how you know he is not a qualified voter.

I saw Mr. Furgerson, I think, bringing him to the polls, and I inferred from his being in Mr. Furgerson's company, together with other Republicans, that he voted the Republican ticket, and their anxiety, when he was objected to by Mr. Jarboe and others, to have him vote.

7th Question.—You state you saw two men register on the day of election who voted the Republican ticket. State who they were, who registered them, and how you know they voted the Republican ticket ; whether any parties named in your testimony as having voted upon the day of election voted without their names being upon the registration list kept or used by the Judges of the Election ?

To the best of my recollection they were Charles Johnson and Payton Powell. They were registered by Walter Griffin, the Register of the District, and they were with the Republicans. Mr. Robey and other Republicans insisted upon their being registered. I know of no parties who voted without their names being upon the registration books. Did not see the inside of any of the tickets of the above-named parties at the time they voted. I saw some of their tickets just immediately before.　　　　　　　　　　JOHN A. FRASER.

Test : James Harris.

Thereupon the taking of this testimony is adjourned until to-morrow morning at 9 o'clock A. M.

December 23d, 1873.

Met pursuant to adjournment.

DEPOSITION No. 7.

JOHN W. MEDLEY, having been first duly sworn, deposed as follows:

By Mr. Brooke:

1st Question.—State your name, age, occupation, residence, and in what election district you voted on the 4th of November, 1873.

My name is John W. Medley; age, 28; clerk under Mr. Brooke in the Clerk's office; residence, Upper Marlboro', and voted in the Third Election District of Prince George's County.

2d Question.—Do you or not know of non-residents of the county or State, or unpardoned convicts, who voted with the Republican party at the election held on the 4th of November, 1873, and how long since each of said parties removed from the county, and where do they now reside?

Yes, I do know of several non-residents, namely, Charles Marshall, Sam. Williams, George Bowling, William Henry Queen, H. Eugene Brooke, Albert Brooke and William Orme. I believe all of them have been out of the county over a year, and some of them for two or three years; and I believe they all reside in the District of Columbia. I know positively that several of them do. I know that Mark Johnson, an unpardoned convict, and Nace Bell, also an unpardoned convict, voted at the said election.

Cross-examined by Mr. Merrick, counsel for Mr. Widdicombe:

1st Question.—How do you know that Charles Marshall, Sam. Williams, George Bowling, William Henry Queen, H. Eugene Brooke, Albert Brooke and William Orme are non-residents of the county and State, and have been for a year? And do you know whether their removal from the county was permanent or not?

I believe that Charles Marshall has not resided in the county for more than a year, and that his coming into the county to vote was the first time I had seen him for more than a year, and he also heard that he had said on the night before the election, or the morning of, I am not certain which, that he resided in Washington ; he did not say so to me, nor did I hear him say so. Sam. Williams, with his family, moved from here to the District of Columbia in the fall of 1872. I know this because he told me that he was going there to live. I believe I saw him the morning he started. This was told me, I think, in the fall of 1872, and does not know whether it was early or late in the fall. George Bowling moved from here, to the best of my recollection, about two years ago, and has since then resided in the District of Columbia ; I have seen him there frequently ; he has told me that he was keeping house there, and I know that he has never been back to the place where he formerly resided within the last year, except on one or two occasions, one of which was to nurse a gentleman in a case of sickness, and perhaps on a matter of business he may have been back. William H. Queen has not lived in this place for more than a year, to the best of my knowledge. H. Eugene Brooke has never, in my recollection, lived in this town permanently, and I know positively that he has not lived here for more than a year ; he once had a sign stuck out in this place as an insurance agent, but that was two or three years ago, and he then claimed his residence in the Fourth Election District of Prince George's County. I know that he does not reside in said county, because he has been doing business in Washington and St. Mary's County, and has his family in Washington and elsewhere out of Prince George's County. I know that Albert Brooke has resided out of said county more than a year, because he lived in Washington and St. Mary's County. William Orme is a non-resident, because he went away to the District of Columbia more than a year ago, and I have not seen him back since that time, until the election. I believe that when they left here they left with the intention of remaining away permanently. My reason for knowing that Sam. Williams has removed permanently is that he told me that he intended to go to Washington to live. I do not, of my own knowledge, know that the above-named parties have removed permanently from the county or not.

2d Question.—How do you know that Charles Marshall, Sam. Williams, George Bowling, Wm. H. Queen, H. Eugene Brooke, Albert Brooke and William Orme voted the Republican ticket?

Because I know that they belong to the Republican party, and have heard Mr. H. Eugene Brooke and George Bowling say that they were Republicans. I did not see the tickets voted by any of the above-named parties.

3d Question.—Have not all the parties, mentioned by you as non-residents, been voting regularly at the elections held in Prince George's County?

Most of them have.

4th Question.—Name those that have been voting in the county to your knowledge?

All except Charles Marshall and Wm. Orme, and they may have, though I do not know it.

5th Question.—Were you or not instrumental in having the name of any of the parties, mentioned by you as non-residents, kept upon the books of registration? If yea; state who the parties were.

I was acting as clerk to Mr. Wm. B. Bowie, the Register for Marlboro' District; a discussion arose about striking the names of H. Eugene Brooke 'and George Bowling from the books of registration; it was objected that if their names were stricken off, it might raise the question of the legality of one Democrat being kept on said books; and whilst I believed them both to be non-residents, I advised that they should not be struck off for the reason given above. The name of the Democrat referred to in the above discussion was Daniel Clarke. I never had any doubt myself about the said Daniel Clarke being a resident, but to avoid raising any question as to the legality of residence, I thought it better to keep the others on.

6th Question.—What do you mean when you say that Mack Johnson and Nace Bell voted with the Republican party?

I mean to say that they voted the Republican ticket; being identified with the Republican party.

7th Question.—How do you know they voted the Republican ticket?

Because I believe that they are identified with the Republican party. I did not see either of the tickets voted by the above-named parties. I know that they are unpardoned convicts, because no certificates of pardon have been filed in the office of the Clerk of the Circuit Court for Prince George's County, it being the court in which they were convicted. I know that they were convicted there, having seen Mack Johnson tried, and have seen the record of the conviction of Nace Bell. Mack Johnson was convicted of larceny and sentenced to the county jail for a short time; does not know how long. I do not know positively for what Nace Bell was tried or what was his sentence; thinks he was tried for larceny and sentenced to the penitentiary.

JOHN W. MEDLEY.

Test: James Harris.

Deposition No. 8.

William A. Jarboe, being duly sworn, deposed as follows:

1st Question.—State your name, age, occupation, residence and in what election district you voted on the 4th of November, 1873?

My name is William A. Jarboe; age, 53; I am treasurer of this county; I reside in Surratt's District; voted in the Ninth Election District of Prince George's County on the 4th of November, 1873, at the election held there on that day.

2d Question.—Do you know of any non-residents of the county or State, or unpardoned convicts, who voted with the Republican party at the election held on the 4th day of November, 1873, and how long since each of said parties removed from this county, and where do they now reside?

I know of one gentleman, named John McKelly, who told me that he had removed from this county. It was during the last day of the last registration he heard that his name was stricken off the registration books and was on his way down to have it put on again. He said he was going to vote for some of the Commissioners on the Democratic ticket. He said he would like to vote for Mr. Daniel Clarke, who was a candidate upon the Democratic ticket, but he could not. I know of George Locker, who was sent to the penitentiary, but do not know whether he has been pardoned or not; he voted an open Republican ticket on the 4th of November, 1873. John McNally was not living in the county last year. I do not know how long he has been living out of the county. He voted at the election in Surratt's District at the election on the 4th of November, 1873.

3d Question.—Do you know of any interference by candidates or other parties, on the day of the election, with any voter or voters? If yea, state whether you know of any intimidation of said voters at said election.

I saw no interference on the part of the Democrats or Republicans at our polls, except that the Republicans pressed up to the polls and held possession of the polls, until they got through voting, for an hour or two ; I do not know of any intimidation used on the day of election.

4th Question.—Do you know of any intimidation being used before the day of election?

I was told by three or four that they wanted to vote the Democratic ticket, but they were afraid to do so. One of them, a colored man who formerly belonged to me, came to me at twelve or one o'clock the night before the election, and told me that he wanted to vote the Democratic ticket, and said if he did they would kill him. I assured him that no one should hurt him.

5th Question.—Do you or do you not know of any qualified voters of Prince George's County who were prevented from voting, at said election, for the Democratic ticket? If yea, give their names.

A man named Samuel J. Allen, in Surratt's District, offered to vote on the day of election. The Judges refused to receive his vote because his name was not on the registered list. The said Allen insisted on voting, stating to the Judges that he had never removed from the district. I know that the said Allen resides in said district, and have seen him vote there. He said he wanted to vote the Democratic ticket, but was not allowed, by the Judges, to do so. Captain B. F. Gwynn and his son, Eddie Gwynn, wanted to vote the Democratic ticket, and were anxious to have their names retained on the registration books, but the Register refused to do so, although they claimed their residence in that district. Mr. Gwynn came down for the purpose of seeing the Register about keeping his name upon the books. Mr. Gwynn requested me to see the Register and to ask him that his and his son's names be kept on. I did see him, and he refused to register them.

6th Question.—Are you or are you not acquainted with James Young? If yea, where does he reside?

I have seen him, and heard him say that he had resided in Spalding's District, but then lived in the Ninth ; that was on the day of election, at the polls, about eleven o'clock. The said James Young offered to vote. I objected, stating to the Judges of the Election that he had been transferred to Marlboro' District. Mr. Griffin, the Register, stated that his name had been stricken off the registration books for the Ninth District. After insisting that he was entitled to vote, the Judges of the Election allowed him to vote, but Mr. Griffin, the Register, objected to it. The Judges of the Election allowed his name to be put on the list of the registered voters, but does not know who wrote his name. I do not know whether he was a qualified voter or not.

Cross-examined :

1st Question.—State if, in the conversation with John McNally, referred to in your testimony in chief, he told you whether or not he claimed his residence in Prince George's County ?

He stated that he desired to claim his residence in this county, and he had removed his family to Washington, but wished still to vote in this county.

2d Question.—State whether you examined the open ticket voted by George Locker, and whether you can say none of the Republican names on said ticket had been scratched off ?

I examined his ticket closely, and can say that none of the Republican names were scratched off. I had occasion to do this, because he had been stating for more than a year that he should vote the Democratic ticket.

3d Question.—Do you or not know where B. F. Gwynn and son, referred to in your testimony, are now residing ? If yea, state how long they have resided there.

They have resided in Baltimore City for two or three years, but they voted in the county two years ago. I don't know whether they voted here last year. They were not at the polls of the election held on the 4th November, 1873.

WM. A. JARBOE.

Test : James Harris.

DEPOSITION No. 9.

CHARLES C. HILL, after being duly sworn, deposes as follows :
By Mr. Magruder, counsel for Mr. Brooke :

1st Question.—State your name, age, occupation and residence, and in what Election District did you vote on the 4th of November, 1873 ?

My name is Charles C. Hill; age, 52 years; occupation, farmer; residence in Prince George's County, and voted in Marlboro' Election District of Prince George's County.

2d Question.—Do you or do you not know of any minors who voted with the Republican party at said election ? If yea, give their names.

I was told that Tom Holland's son, a colored boy who goes by the name of " Fellow," voted here. I say he is a minor, because I have a register, kept by my father, and the name of Teresa, a sister of said boy, called " Fellow," will be twenty years old next January, 1874; she is the oldest child, and I think the boy " Fellow" is next to her in age. I suppose he is about 19 years old; am positive he is not twenty-one. I do not know how said party voted or whether he voted at all; nor do I know his name other than stated above, but he is the child of Tom Holland. I was told by the Registrar that he registered him on the faith of a letter from Mr. Tolson.

CHARLES C. HILL.

Test: JAMES HARRIS.

DEPOSITION No. 10.

BASIL T. BROWN, being duly sworn, deposes as follows :
By Mr. Magruder, Jr., counsel for Mr. Brooke :

1st Question.—State your name, age, occupation and place of residence, and in what Election District you voted on the 4th day of November, 1873 ?

My name is Basil T. Brown; age, 34 years; occupation, farmer, and reside in Marlboro' District, and voted in Upper Marlboro' on the 4th of November, 1873, at the election held on that day.

2d Question.—Do you or do you not know of any interference, by candidates or other parties, with any voter or voters at said election, and state, further, whether you know of any intimidation of voters at said election ?

On the day of the election, Mr. Widdicombe, who was a candidate for the Clerk of the County, stood in the Court House door and made parties show him their tickets; from those who had not Republican but had Democratic tickets he took the Democratic tickets away and gave them Republican tickets that had the figure three (3) on them; does not know whether the figure was on the outside or inside of said tickets. He put the Democratic tickets in his pocket that he took from the voters. He does not know of any intimidation of voters on the day of election except about these tickets.

Cross-examined by Merrick, counsel for Mr. Widdicombe:

1st Question.—State whether the parties, at whose tickets Mr. Widdicombe looked, showed them willingly, or whether he used any force or violence to obtain the same?

He would not let them enter the door to the polls until they showed their tickets. Mr. Widdicombe was on the second step of the outside Court House door. He used no violence or force except to take the parties by the arm and requested them to show their tickets. I do not think that any one could get in the Court House door without showing his ticket. I did not see any one go in the door without showing Mr. Widdicombe his ticket.

2d Question.—How long did Mr. Widdicombe remain at the door looking at these tickets?

He remained there about two hours in the morning; shortly after Mr. Widdicombe left the door, I went out of Marlboro'.

3d Question.—After Mr. Widdicombe looked at these tickets, did he remain at the door or did he go with the parties to the ballot-box?

He remained at the door.

4th Question.—Do you know of any one prevented on that day from voting by Mr. Widdicombe because said party, or parties, would not show his ballot, or any other cause?

I do not, except that the parties had to show their tickets.

5th Question.—How do you know that the tickets taken by Mr. Widdicombe were Democratic tickets, and did you see the face of the same, and how do you know the tickets given by Mr. Widdicombe in their stead were Republican tickets?

Because I was close enough to see and read them, and did see the face of all the tickets that Mr. Widdicombe took from the parties. I could tell that the tickets given in the place of the others were Republican tickets by the figure three being printed on them, and Mr. Widdicombe took the tickets from his pocket.

6th Question.—State how many Democratic tickets you saw Mr. Widdicombe take from voters, and how many Republican tickets you saw him give in their stead.

I saw him take three Democratic tickets and give three Republican tickets in their place. Those were all the Democratic tickets I saw him take.

7th Question.—Could not the parties from whom you saw Mr. Widdicombe take the Democratic tickets have procured other Democratic tickets on their way to the ballot-box, or at the ballot-box, if they chose?

I do not know whether they could or not.

8th Question.—Could not said parties have refrained from voting the tickets given them by Mr. Widdicombe, if they chose?

I don't know about that.

BASIL T. BROWN.

Test : JAMES HARRIS.

DEPOSITION No. 11.

JOSEPH K. ROBERTS, JR., first being duly sworn, testified as follows :

By Mr. Magruder, Jr., counsel for Mr. Brooke :

1st Question.—State your name, age, occupation and residence, and state in what election district you voted on the day of election, November 4th, 1873.

My name is Joseph K. Roberts; age, 32 years; occupation, attorney-at-law; residence is in Marlboro' District, Prince George's County, where I voted on the 4th day of November, 1873.

2d Question.—Do you know of any non-residents of the said county or State who voted with the Republican party at the said election, and how long since each of said parties removed from said county, and where do they now reside?

I saw William Orme, who has not been a resident of this county, to the best of my knowledge, for two years, and who told me this fall, prior to the election, that he resided in

Washington, vote here. I did not read his ticket, but from the appearance of the ticket, and the company in which he voted, I think I could safely infer that it was a Republican ticket. I protested against his voting at the time to him, and told him I did not think he was entitled to vote in this county. I saw no other non-resident deposit their ballots, but I am satisfied that Mr. Eugene Brooke, Mr. Albert Brooke and George Bowling, colored, have not resided in this county within twelve months before said election.

3d Question.—Do you know of any interference by candidates or other parties with any voter or voters at said election, and state further whether you know of any intimidation of voters at the same?

I reached the polls the election day about half-past nine o'clock; when I got there I found the front door of the Court House leading to the polls, the polls being held in the Court House, blockaded up entirely by a mass and crowd of colored people, seeking their turn to vote; that crowd extended from the Court House door, occupied the entire vestibule of the Court House, between the outer and inner door, and more than half way of the Court House yard, a distance of about fifteen or twenty yards. It was utterly impossible for any voter other than those in those ranks to deposit a vote, except an occasional white voter, who was permitted by the guards there stationed to approach the ballot-box through the rear door of the Court House. Those guards were there for the purpose of preventing persons from entering the Court House through that door. I at once saw the injustice that such proceeding would work. I saw voters, both white and black, who professed a desire to vote the Democratic ticket, who were unable to gain admission to the polls at that time. I then went, together with one or two other gentlemen, and suggested to the Judges of the Election that it was impossible to have a fair election in the manner things were then conducted, and suggested that it was but fair and proper that admission of voters should be permitted through the rear door of the Court House. I thought that such had been the custom heretofore. The Judges, and particularly Mr. Flint, one of the Judges of the Election, did not seem willing to grant this permission, stating that they had determined to

permit voters only through the front door of the Court House.
I then asked them to have the vestibule of the Court House
cleared so that both parties might have equal access to the
polls. Such an order was issued to the officers deputized for
the occasion. I then went out of the Court House and around
to the front door, where I saw Mr. Wedding, one of the officers, attempting to carry out the order, but who most signally
failed. I approached him and told him that we required that
that order should be carried into effect. He told me it was
impossible for him to do it. I told him that he was an officer
of the law; that it was his duty to do it, if necessary by force.
He said he did not wish to kill any body, and could not do it
unless he did, or words to that effect. I then went with Mr.
William B. Hill, Charles Hill, I think, and one or two other
gentlemen, back into the Court House, told the Judges what
Mr. Wedding had stated; told them that free access to the
polls was impossible, and that unless the rear door of the
Court House was opened so that voters might approach the
polls through it, that many parties would leave before voting,
and that we would not submit to the election. I then suggested that they allow five voters to approach at one door and
vote, and at the other, alternately; such an order was passed,
and then, about eleven o'clock, the rear door was opened and
free access was permitted in the manner above indicated.
From that time the balloting was properly conducted. I also
saw Captain Widdicombe, who was standing near the ballot-
box most of the forenoon of the day, examine the tickets of the
colored voters as they approached the ballot-box. It was unusual, and I took particular notice of it for some time. I
finally approached some of the parties whose tickets he was
then examining, and who appeared to me to think he had a
right to do it, and told them Mr. Widdicombe had no right
to examine their tickets; and asked them why they were
showing them to him; they replied he asked them to do so.
I again told them he had no right to examine their tickets.
He replied that he had a right to examine them if they
thought proper to show them to him. I told him yes, he had
a right to examine them if they thought proper voluntarily to
show them, but he had no right to stand at the ballot-box and
demand them to show their tickets. Mr. Widdicombe used

.no violence to make the party show him their tickets, but the impression made upon my mind by the peculiar manner in which he approached the colored voters and asked to see their tickets, was that they thought it was their duty and they were obliged to do it. I will give a reason why this impression was made upon me. I saw a young colored man approach the ballot-box to vote; was told that he resided at Mr. Charles C. Hill's; John W. Belt, of Oak Grove, was at that time standing with his back to me and the ballot-box, conversing with some one, and I think with Mr. Richard Sasscer. I saw Mr. Widdicombe ask to see his ticket, and he handed it to him; just then Mr. Belt turned and asked this man if he had voted, and he said no, and approaching Mr. Widdicombe, said, you have my ticket. Mr. Widdicombe handed him a ticket which looked to me very much like a Republican ticket, though I did not see the names. The Judges of the Election were calling upon him to vote; he walked up at the instant, deposited the ticket Mr. Widdicombe had handed him, and turned away. I heard Mr. Belt say something to him about voting, but I did not catch his remark, when Mr. Widdicombe also walked away, and we picked up from where he had been standing a Democratic ticket, which Mr. Belt said was this man's ticket; it was rolled up and had every appearance of a ticket to be voted. So far as I know there was no mark on the ticket to designate that from any other Democratic ticket, but, from surrounding circumstances, I judged that it was this man's ticket.

4th Question.—Do you know in what election district of said county the same Robert S. Widdicombe is a registered voter, and whether or not he voted there at said election?

Capt. Widdicombe is a resident of Second Election District of said county. I am sure he did not vote in that district; he was in the Third District all day.

Cross-examined:

1st Question.—Do you know how these guards came to be stationed at the back door?

I presume by the Judges of the Election; they were residents of the district, and deputized for the occasion to prevent voting through the back door.

2d Question.—Do you know whether William Orme, Eugene Brooke, Albert Brooke and George Bowling have removed permanently from the county, and what reply, if any, the said Orme made to you on the day of the election when you protested against his right to vote?

I know that William Orme told me that he was living in Washington City; I know that he has been absent from the county about two years; I know that George Bowling has been a resident of Washington City since, I think, January, 1871, if what he told me was true. He gave me his number of residence in Washington to write to him. Mr. Eugene Brooke and Albert Brooke reside in Washington, if general reputation can be relied on. I do not know personally where they reside, nor do I know the intention of any of the said parties.

3d Question.—Was there or not ample opportunity and time between the opening and closing of the polls on the 4th November, 1873, in Marlboro' District, for every one wishing to vote to have done so if they were disposed to wait?

There was ample opportunity for voters to vote, but the manner in which the voting was conducted in early morning was undoubtedly calculated to influence and intimidate voting in favor of the Republican ticket.

JOSEPH K. ROBERTS.

Test: JAMES HARRIS.

Thereupon the taking of this testimony is adjourned until to-morning morning, 9½ o'clock, A. M.

DECEMBER 23d, 1873.

Met pursuant to adjournment.

DEPOSITION No. 12.

JAMES H. RITCHIE, first being duly sworn, deposes and says: Mr. Merrick, counsel for Mr. Widdicombe, after the first question was propounded, and before it was answered, objected to the examination of Mr. Ritchie, for the reason that his name does not appear in the list of witnesses in the notice served upon Mr. Widdicombe, as required by Section 59, Article 35, of the Code.

1st Question.—State your name, age, occupation, place of residence and in what election district you voted on the 4th November, 1873?

My name is James H. Ritchie; age, 27 years; occupation, Deputy Clerk under Mr. Brooke; reside in Upper Marlboro', and voted in the Third Election District of Prince George's County, on the 4th November, 1873.

2d Question.—Do you or do you not know of any non-residents of Prince George's County or the State of Maryland who voted with the Republican party at said election? If yea, state how many and give their names; state all you know about it.

I know one Samuel Williams, a colored man, who told me himself that he resided in Washington City; he told me this on the day of the election, and that he voted the Republican ticket; and also that he had voted in Washington City; he did not say when he had voted in Washington; I think he left here last winter.

3d Question.—Did you or did you not leave a notice of the taking of testimony, while acting as Deputy Sheriff in this case, at the residence of Robert S. Widdicombe? If yea, how long did you remain there for the purpose of giving said notice?

Mr. Merrick here excepted to the interrogatory, because it is not embraced in the notice as one of the things to be proved by the Contestant.

I did leave a notice at Mr. Widdicombe's house with his wife, or with a lady I supposed to be his wife. I remained at the house for perhaps a half hour. She told me that Mr. Widdicombe was in Washington; I went to Washington the same day and saw Mr. Widdicombe, and told him that I had been to his house and left a notice there for him: I told him the notice contained the list of witnesses and what Mr. Brooke expected to prove by them.

Cross-examined by Mr. Merrick: •

1st Question.—State, if you please, in whose hand-writing was the notice you left at Mr. Widdicombe's house.

Notice I left with Mr. Widdicombe was in the hand-writing of Mr. Brooke.

2d Question.—Look at the paper now shown you and state

in whose hand-writing the same is, and whether or not it is the notice left by you at Mr. Widdicombe's house.

It is in the hand-writing of Mr. Henry Brooke, and is the paper I left at Mr. Widdicombe's house.

3d *Question.*—Look at said notice and say whether or not your name appears in the list of witnesses there given.

It does not.

JAMES H. RITCHIE.

Test: JAMES HARRIS.

DEPOSITION NO. 13.

JEREMIAH COFFREN, being duly sworn, deposes and says:

1st *Question.*—State your name, age, occupation, place of residence, and in what election district you voted on the 4th of November, 1873.

My name is Jeremiah Coffren; age, 30 years; occupation, farmer; residence, Prince George's County, and voted in the Fourth Election District of said county.

2d *Question.*—Are you or are you not the Officer of Registration of said election district?

I am.

3d *Question.*—Do you or do you not know of any minors who voted at the polls in said election district on said election day? If yea, state how many, give their names, and how you know them to have been minors on said election day. Did or did not said parties vote with the·Republican party on that day?

I can't state definitely that they are minors or not, but will give you my reasons for thinking they were. Ambrose Carroll and Hamilton Carroll I believe to be minors; did not see either of them vote; Ambrose Carroll told me he voted at the polls in Nottingham. My reasons for believing them to be minors are because I hired them from their father, Robert Carroll, as minors, who always received their hire; at times he told me to pay the hire to themselves. I believe them to be minors for this reason: They came to me to be registered; I refused them, unless they would produce evidence that they were twenty-one years old. They produced then their father and mother. I asked them why that they now say (meaning the day of registration) that the said boys are twenty-one, when they had been saying all the year that said boys were not twenty-one. They stated to me then that said boys are twins; were born at the time Dr. John H. Skinner was away on the trial of Dr. Worthington for the shooting of Charles Crook. They said that that trial was in 1851. I would not register them upon that testimony, and they then swore that the said boys were twenty-one years of age. I then registered them. Their mother came to me on the Saturday before the election day and asked me could I strike their names from the books of registration; that she had been satisfied that she had made a mistake in their age; she was satisfied that they were not old enough to vote, and hereafter she would do what she thought was right, and not take the advice of others. The boy, Ambrose Carroll, also requested me to strike his name off the books of registration. I told them that the books of registration were in the Clerk's Office of the county, and I could not strike them off. I told them that I had only the certified copy in the house, and that I could not take them off one book without I had the power to take them off all. Ambrose then said that he would not vote; would not go to the polls. Ambrose told me since the election that he voted for Mr. Widdicombe. I did not see Hamilton at the election, that I remember.

Cross-examined by Mr. Merrick:

1st Question.—Do you or not know that the two minors alluded to above, after being registered by you, were told or threatened by any person or persons that if they voted they would be prosecuted for perjury, and whether or not any efforts were made to deter the said parties from voting? If yea, state by whom.

I do not. They asked me what would be the result in the case if they did not vote, and I told them that if they did not vote, it was likely to remain quietly as it was. To the above questions he answered, I do not.

2d Question.—Is what you say about their ages since you registered them, derived from hearsay or actual knowledge?

Part of it is derived from others, and part from the Clerk's Office. I say that this trial, to the best of my knowledge, took place in 1853.

3d Question.—Who showed you the information you derived in the Clerk's Office?

Mr. A. T. Brooke and Mr. Henry Brooke.

4th Question.—Do you know that that was the record of the trial of Mr. Worthington for the shooting of Crook, except from what Mr. A. T. and Henry Brooke told you?

I do not.

5th Question.—How came Ambrose Carroll to tell you that he voted for Mr. Widdicombe? and do you or not know person or persons voting the Republican ticket, but voting for Mr. Henry Brooke for Clerk?

It was in a general conversation with the hands that worked with me, that I asked him how he voted. I do not know any person voting the Republican ticket, and voting for Mr. Henry Brooke for Clerk.

6th Question.—Did you or not, on the day of election, tell Mr. H. Eugene Brooke that those parties were entitled to vote?

I did not.

7th Question.—Do you or do you not know of any person or persons who, from intimidation or fear of violence, were prevented from voting on the day of election?

I do not.

JEREMIAH COFFREN.

Test : JAMES HARRIS.

DEPOSITION No. 14.

JOHN S. RITCHIE, being duly sworn, deposes as follows:

1st Question.—State your name, age, occupation, place of residence, and where you voted on the election held on the 4th November, 1873?

My name is John S. Ritchie; age, 56; occupation, farmer in Bladensburg District, Prince George's County. I voted in said district, being No. 2.

2d Question.—Do you or do you not know of any qualified voters who were prevented from voting at said election for the Democratic candidates? If yea, please give their names, and state where they resided on the day of election.

I do; Charles Walker and John Hays; they are white. They resided in the Second District of said county. They

offered to vote, and their ballots were refused by the Judges
of the Election, because their names did not appear upon the
list of registered qualified voters.   I know that Mr. Hays is a
qualified voter, because I have seen him vote there time after
time, and I don't believe he ever voted anywhere else.   He
has been residing in said district for fifteen or twenty years,
and still resides there.   Mr. Walker has been residing in said
district for three years.   They both told me that they wanted
to vote the Democratic ticket.

Cross-examined:

1st *Question.*—State, if you please, if the Officers of Registration and the Judges of Election in Bladensburg District
are Democrats or Republicans.

I suppose the Registration Officer is a Democrat; I believe
two of the Judges of Election are Democrats, and the other
a Republican.

2d *Question.*—Do you know why the names of Charles
Walker and John Hays were not upon the registration list?

I do not.

JOHN S. ᕮ RITCHIE.
<small>HIS</small>
<small>MARK</small>

Test: JAMES HARRIS.

DEPOSITION No. 15.

RICHARD PEACH, being duly sworn, deposes as follows:

1st *Question.*—State your name, age, occupation, place of
residence, and in what election district you voted on the 4th
day of November, 1873 (the election day).

My name is Richard Peach; age, 40 years; occupation,
farmer; I reside in Queen Ann District, Prince George's
County, where I voted on the day of election.

2d *Question.*—Do you or do you not know of any qualified
voters who were prevented from voting for the Democratic
candidates by intimidation at said election?

I know of two, who stated to me that it was through fear that
they did not vote the Democratic ticket.   One of the parties
is named Elsey Tilghman, and the other Jacob Oakey.   Elsey
Tilghman voted, and told me that the Democratic ticket that
he had was taken from him by violence, and another put into

his hand; he did not state what kind of ticket was put into his hand. The Democratic ticket was taken from him by the crowd, by whom he meant the Republicans. Oakey did not vote, and he stated to me that it was through fear and intimidation that he did not vote. He did not state by whom he was intimidated; that is, by no separate individual, but by the opposing party, meaning the Republican party.

Cross-examined:

1st Question.—State, if you please, whether you gave tickets to either of these men; if yea, where you gave them, and with whom they went to the polls, and how you know that Oakey did not vote?

I gave Democratic tickets to both of these men, at the Governor's Bridge, Anne Arundel County, at their request. Jacob Oakey came to the polls by himself. I do not know who came with Tilghman. I know that Oakey did not vote, because I was one of the Judges of Election.

2d Question.—State if there was not ample opportunity and time between the opening and closing of the polls on the 4th of November, 1873, for any one wishing to vote, to do so?

There was. Not to my knowledge did Oakey offer to vote. I do not know, of my own knowledge, of any person prevented by violence or intimidation from voting on the day of election.

3d Question.—Did you mark either of the tickets given by you to the above-named parties, or any other tickets given by you to voters, so that you might know whether they had been voted or not?

I did mark the tickets given by me to the said parties by writing on them the words "true blue."

4th Question.—Did you examine the tickets after the polls were closed to see whether those tickets had been voted or not, and if so, did you find them?

I examined every ticket that was taken out of the poll-box for that purpose, and did not find them.

5th Question.—State whether, after failing to find these tickets, you asked the above-named parties why they had not voted them, and if the statement made by them, as given above, was in response to such inquiry?

I did ask them, and their statement was in reply to that question. These parties reside in Queen Ann District, on Dr. Joseph I. Duvall's place.

RICHARD PEACH.

Test: JAMES HARRIS.

Thereupon adjourned until Friday, December 26th, 1873, at 11 o'clock A. M.

FRIDAY, DECEMBER 26th, 1873.

Met pursuant to adjournment.

DEPOSITION No. 16.

DR. FREDERICK SASSCER, being duly sworn, deposed as follows:

1st Question.—State your name, age, occupation, place of residence, and where you voted on the 4th day of November, 1873.

My name is Frederick Sasscer; age, 46; occupation, farmer; residence, Upper Marlboro'; I voted in the Third Election District of Prince George's County.

2d Question.—Do you or do you not know of any non-residents of this county or State who voted with the Republican party at said election; if yea, please give their names, how many there are, how long since each of said parties left this county, and where do they now reside?

I think I know three who are non-residents, viz: Charles Marshall, David White and Peter Greenleaf. Charles Marshall, who lived with me, left the county, I am certain, at least two years ago and went to Washington, where he now resides; the reason I know, he told me the last week in conversation with him in Washington, that he still lived there. David White and Peter Greenleaf lived with Mr. Richard B. B. Chew, and left him one year ago and went to Washington to live. · I can't say positively that the last two voted the Republican ticket, but supposed they did, as they were with the body of colored Republican voters until the mass of voting was over. Charles Marshall admitted to me that he voted the Republican ticket.

3d Question.—Do you know of any interference by candidates or other parties with any voter or voters at said election? State further, whether or not you know of any intimidation of voters at said election? If yea, state it fully?

I know of no interference by any candidate, but I think the interference of parties from Washington went very far to prejudice the result of the voting in this district. One party, who had always said that he intended to vote the Democratic ticket, and was going up to the Court House with me to vote, was taken away by a colored Federal office holder and placed within the ranks of colored men at the Court House door, pushed into the Court House, where I could not possibly get at the time, and voted. His name is Joseph Galloway. There was a colored man from Washington City haranguing for nearly an hour and a half in front of the Court House; the character of his speech, I think, prevented many from voting the Democratic ticket who would otherwise have done so. The said Joseph Galloway was with force jerked from me. There was fully one dozen colored men from Washington, including the band, which was playing at the time, who were in the Court House yard manipulating the voters.

4th Question.—Was or was not said election fairly conducted at your polls, in your opinion, and was the result a fair expression of the sentiments of the voters?

I do not think the election was fairly conducted, nor do I think that the result was a fair expression of the sentiments of the voters.

Cross-examined:

1st Question.—Do you know that Charles Marshall, David White and Peter Greenleaf have been out of the county for more than a year, and, if so, whether it was their purpose to reside permanently out of the county?

I know that Charles Marshall has been out of the county for more than a year, and when he left me he stated his purpose was to reside in Washington. I do not know that the other two have been away quite twelve months, but, before they left, I wanted to hire them; they told me that they intended to leave the county and reside in Washington. It has been a year since the above conversation, and they may have remained some time in the county after the conversation without my knowledge.

2d Question.—Do you know whether either of the parties referred to voted in any other place since they left?

I do not.

3d Question.—Do you know whether the names of the parties referred to appeared upon the list of qualified voters furnished to the Judges of Election?

I do not.

4th Question.—Do you know whether or not they voted the Republican ticket?

I only supposed so from the facts and reasons given in my answer to the second interrogatory in chief.

5th Question.—Do you know of any objection, on the day of election, to those parties voting because they had resided out of the district?

I do not.

6th Question.—Do you know whether Joseph Galloway resisted or objected to go with the parties who took him from you on the day of the election, and whether or not he voted the Republican ticket?

He did not resist; he was too much frightened to do so; I know not what ticket he voted.

7th Question.—Had you any conversation with Joseph Galloway prior to his being taken from you, and whether, at your request, he had consented to vote the Democratic ticket?

I heard him say frequently, prior to the election, that he intended to vote the Democratic ticket. On the morning of the election I saw this colored Federal office-holder talking with him at the Court House fence. I went to him then and asked him to vote, probably I took hold of him by the arm, and he readily came with me.

8th Question.—What was the name of this colored Federal office-holder, and was he a voter in this district?

I do not know his name; I heard him say he was a Federal office-holder; I am certain he never was a voter in this district.

9th Question.—State whether or not it was after you had taken Joseph Galloway from the colored Federal office-holder that he took him from you?

It was after he left the place.

10th Question.—You say that there was a colored man haranguing the voters; state how far it was from the polls his speech was being made, and whether you noted his remarks and what the substance of them was?

I suppose he was about ten or fifteen feet from the walls of the Court House ; he was a good speaker, and, among other things which I heard him say, "that the angels of the murdered colored people of the South were looking down from Heaven upon them, and if they voted the Democratic ticket that they could not expect to join them in Heaven." The ranting of his speech was more in the character of a Methodist preacher.

11th Question.—Was there not ample time and opportunity for all voters, between the opening and closing of the polls on the 4th day of November, 1873, to cast their votes, if they wished to remain during the day until the crowd had voted?

I think all who remained in town had time to vote.

12th Question.—Has it not been usual at all elections since the colored people have been voting, for their vote to be cast in a body during the first hour or two of the election, the white people preferring to wait until the rush was over?

It has been the custom, I believe ; but I never saw so much foreign influence used before to put all other colored people in the body of voters. The white people, I think, have waited more from necessity than choice heretofore.

13th Question.—Do you know of any one who was prevented by violence or force from voting on the 4th day of November, 1873? If so, name him.

I saw this old colored man, Alec Gross, who stated in my hearing that he had been so badly injured in his shoulder that he must go home. I do not know whether he offered to vote. I do not know whether he received those injuries in attempting to vote, of my own knowledge, except from heresay.

14th Question.—Did you use any influence with, or make any promises to Joseph Galloway or others, to induce him or them to vote the Democratic ticket?

I made no promises to any one ; I used no influence, except legitimate.

15th Question.—Were not a majority of the Judges conducting said election Democrats?

I think they were.

16th Question.—Was any complaint made by either of them that the election was not being conducted fairly during the progress of said election?

I did not see either of the Judges that day, except when I voted; I did not talk with them.

17th Question.—Do you know of parties who voted who were Republicans and voted for Mr. Brooke, and whether any inducements were offered them to do so? whether any parties were threatened with a loss of their homes if they did not vote for Mr. Brooke?

I know some Republicans who voted for him, but none from threats or favors granted to do so.

FRED. SASSCER.

Test: James Harris.

Deposition No. 17.

George W. Richardson, being duly sworn, deposed as follows:

1st Question.—State your name, age, occupation, place of residence, and where you voted on the 4th of November, 1873.

My name is George W. Richardson; age, 47; restaurant-keeper; reside in Prince George's County, and voted in the Ninth Election District of said county.

2d Question.—Do you or do you not know of any non-residents of this county or State who voted with the Republican party at said election? If yea, please give their names, and how long since each of said parties removed from the county, and where do they now reside?

I do; John McNally and Frank Allen. They reside in Washington; they both voted on said election day. They both said to me that they voted with the Republican party at said election. Mr. McNally has been gone from the county for two years, and Mr. Allen over two years.

3d Question.—Do you or do you not know of any persons prevented from voting the Democratic ticket in said district by intimidation on said election day? If yea, please name them.

No, sir; not on the day of election.

4th Question.—Do you or not know of any other matter or thing that would be of advantage to the Contestant in this case? If yea, please state it.

I know that Mr. Van Robey, the night before the election, took a man away by force that wished to vote the Democratic ticket.

[The above answer was excepted to by Mr. Widdicombe upon the ground that it was not pertinent to questions contained in the notice of the Contestant.]

5th Question.—Was or was not the said Van Robey a candidate on the Republican ticket? If yea, for what office or position was he running?

He was a candidate on the Republican ticket for the House of Delegates.

Cross-examined:

1st Question.—Did you see either John McNally or Frank Allen vote on said election day, and did you see either of them vote the Republican ticket?

I did not see either of said parties vote on said election day; they had not got there when I left.

2d Question.—Do you know that John McNally and Frank Allen had left the county, at the time of said election, intending to reside permanently elsewhere?

I only know that McNally left the county and took his family with him to Washington to work in the Navy Yard, over two years ago. I do not know what his intentions were. Frank Allen has been working in Washington for over two years.

3d Question.—How do you know that they left the county with their families, with the purpose of residing permanently out of it?

I should think that if a man left the county with his family, that would be his residence where he worked.

4th Question.—Do you know that John McNally and Frank Allen, or either of them, voted elsewhere since you say they left the county. If so, state how you know it?

I do not know.

5th Question.—You say that Mr. Van Robey took a man away the night before the election; state the name of the man, the place where he took him to, and from whom he took him, and whether any violence was used, or any resistance made by the colored man, and how you know that he would have voted the Democratic ticket?

4

I do not know his name; I do not know where he took him to; he took him in his buggy and carried him away. I saw Mr. Robey sitting in his buggy with his pistol cocked and— (Mr. Widdicombe excepts to Mr. Richardson's making this correction in his testimony,)—I saw some three or four razors drawn, and I saw two or three whites put their hands in their pockets—Mr. Wm. Allen for one—but did not draw anything. There was no resistance made by the colored man after they got him in the buggy; they had to pull him in. The colored man told me he was going to vote the Democratic ticket.

6th Question.—Do you know whether this colored man voted the Democratic ticket or not?

I don't know. I supposed he voted the Republican ticket, as he was marched up in the ranks. I did not see him vote or offer to vote.

7th Question.—State whether or not Mr. Jarboe did not ask the colored man if he wanted to vote the Democratic ticket, and assure him, if he did, he would see that he voted it; and that the colored man said he wanted to go with Mr. Robey?

He did, after the row was over, say that he did want to go with Mr. Robey.

8th Question.—Do you know of any one who was prevented by violence or force from voting on the 4th day of November, 1873; if so, name him?

I know of none on the day of election.

9th Question.—Were a majority of the Judges of Election of the Ninth District, Democrats?

They were not. Two were Republicans and one Democrat.

10th Question.—Was there not ample time between the opening and closing of the polls for all qualified voters to deposit their votes, if they were so inclined?

I do not know. I left a short time after 9 o'clock A. M.

Re-called by the Contestant:

1st Question.—Was this unknown man that you have spoken of, at a Democratic meeting or not, and were the razors spoken of, drawn by the parties there first, or by those who came after him?

He was at a Democratic meeting. The razors were drawn by the parties who came after I got there, and who went away following Mr. Robey and the man.

Re-cross-examined :

1st Question.—Was Mr. Jarboe trying to prevent this colored man from getting into the buggy with Mr. Robey?

I did not see him trying to prevent him from getting into the buggy with Mr. Robey ; but Mr. Jarboe said that if he wanted to go with Mr. Robey and vote the Republican ticket, he could go ; if not, Mr. Robey could not take him away. The colored man said he prefered to go with Mr. Robey.

GEORGE W. ☒ RICHARDSON.
HIS
MARK.

Test: JAMES HARRIS.

Thereupon adjourned until to-morrow morning, at 9 o'clock A. M.

———

DECEMBER 27th, 1873.

Met pursuant to adjournment.

DEPOSITION No. 18.

JOHN EARNSHAW, being duly sworn, deposes as follows:

1st Question.—State your name, age, occupation, place of residence, and where you voted on the 4th of November, 1873.

My name is John Earnshaw ; age in May, 53d year ; occupation, farmer ; I reside in Queen Anne District, Prince George's County, and voted in the Seventh Election District.

2d Question.—Do you or do you not know of any qualified voters who were prevented from voting the Democratic ticket at said election? If yea, state their names, and how many there were?

I do ; Oden Williams and Charles Stewart asked me on the morning of the election to give them Democratic tickets ; they wanted to vote the Democratic ticket. Before leaving for the polls, Charlie asked me to fix his ticket so that he could vote the Radical ticket with the exception of Mr. Clarke and Mr. Brooke ; before I got through with fixing his ticket he left, requesting me to give him the ticket at the polls ; when we got to Queen Anne's I found a gang of negroes standing near the polls, that is about fifty yards of the polls ; I saw them hail Oden Williams ; I passed on myself; that is about as far as I know myself up to that time. Some time after, Williams came to me and said they took his ticket away from him and tore it up, and forced him to vote the Radical ticket. Charlie Stewart, the day after the election, I think—it might have been two days after, am not positive—said to me : " I could not get to you at the polls to get that ticket that you promised to give me for fear that they would see me, and I had to vote the Radical ticket." I have a son living in Washington City at this time, John T. Earnshaw, who has always been voting at Queen Anne's ever since he has been a voter ; claims that as his place to vote. His name was stricken from the list some time prior to the election ; he tried to have it put on by writing to Mr. Bowie, the Registrar ; I applied also myself to Mr. Bowie ; both his effort and mine were refused.

Cross-examined :

1st Question.—How do you know that Oden Williams and Charles Stewart were qualified voters, and that their names appeared upon the corrected list of registered voters furnished by the Registrar to the Judges of the Election ?

I do not know that their names were on the list, more than that they were in the habit of voting there ; I believe they are qualified voters ; I did not see them vote.

2d Question.—Were you present at the polls on election day, and did you see either of the parties named above, Oden Williams and Charles Stewart, prevented from voting, or did you see any force used to prevent them from voting ; and if they voted, whether you know of your own knowledge whether they voted the Democratic or Republican ticket ?

I was present ; I saw very little of Oden Williams, but Charles Stewart stood about the polls some time ; I do not know how long ; I did not see either of them prevented from voting ; I saw no violence used towards them ; I did not see either of them vote.

3d Question.—Do you know of any colored men who voted the Democratic ticket, on the day of election, on the 4th day of November, 1873, at the polls of the Seventh Election District, and was any force or violence used to prevent them ?

I did not see those that I allude to vote Democratic tickets.

4th Question.—Did you not solicit Oden Williams and Charles Stewart, and other colored men to vote for Mr. Brooke on the day of election, and did you hold out any inducements to them for so doing ?

I did; I held out no inducements except to say that their interests were mine; I offered no money or pay in any other way.

5th Question.—Will you state wherein your interests and theirs were identical?

I consider that their interests and mine were identical in this way: If they elected an unknown party, taxes might be higher, and affect both me and them.

6th Question.—Is not the Registrar, Richard C. Bowie, a Democrat, and is it not made his duty by law, under a heavy penalty, to strike off the names of every disqualified voter? Did not Mr. Bowie believe your son so disqualified?

I do not know whether he is or not. Mr. Bowie contended that my son had lost his residence by moving to Washington, but my son, who has been living in Washington for a year or more, nearly two years, has always claimed his residence with his father, and has never voted in Washington or made application to register there. He lived in Baltimore two years before he moved to Washington; he moved from Baltimore to my house and stayed there some time. I am not familiar with the law and do not know what the penalty is.

7th Question.—Did your son offer to vote on the day of election, and was his vote refused by the Judges, and, if so, upon what ground?

He did not offer to vote; he knew his name was stricken from the list.

8th Question.—Was there not ample opportunity and time, between the opening and closing of the polls at your election district, on the 4th day of November, 1873, for any one wishing to vote to do so, if he chose to remain during the day and wait until the crowd had voted?

I could not answer that question as to the opening and closing of the polls. I was not there at the opening and left before they closed. There was ample opportunity and time.

9th Question.—Do you know of any one who was prevented by violence or force from voting, and who, in consequence of such violence or force, did not vote at the election on the 4th of November, 1873? If yea, give their name or names.

I do not know of any.

10th Question—Do you know of any one who voted at said

election, in your district or elsewhere in the county, who has not been registered?

I do not.

Re-called by Mr. Brooke:

1st Question.—Do you or do you not know of any threats that were made by any party or parties at said election to influence any voter or voters in casting his or their tickets? If yea, please state all about said threats.

I do. During the day I heard one man say, "all who voted Democratic tickets would have to be wiped out; we will settle it at the mouth of the cannon." I do not know the man; he was a colored man, very black.

Re-cross-examined:

1st Question.—To whom were these remarks addressed, and was it in front of and close to the voting place, and did these remarks, to your knowledge, prevent any one from voting, and if so, name him or them?

They were addressed to a crowd of colored men standing around; there may have been a hundred. It was directly in front of the polls, about sixty feet from the polls. I do not know that these remarks prevented any one from voting.

JOHN EARNSHAW.

Test: JAMES HARRIS.

DEPOSITION No. 19.

WASHINGTON JOHNSON, being duly sworn, deposes as follows:

1st Question.—State your name, age, occupation, place of residence, and where you voted on the 4th day of November, 1873?

My name is Washington Johnson; do not exactly know my age, about 24 or 25; laborer, on the farm at Captain Gardner's; voted here, at the Court House, at the last election.

2d Question.—Were you or not prevented from voting a Democratic ticket, or for Henry Brooke, by intimidation, or induced to vote the Republican ticket at said election by fear, and state all the circumstances attending the case?

I was not prevented from voting. The day that I came down here to vote I had told Mr. Brooke that I was going to vote for him, and when I came from home I brought my ticket with me; it was one of his tickets that I brought from home, and I saw Mr. Tom Clagett after I came here, and he called me aside and asked me to let him see my ticket, and he looked at it and he said that was all right, and he told me to go on and vote that ticket, that it was all right; and the reason that I did not vote it, and after I came out by the gate and left Mr. Clagett, there was a whole crowd of fellows got around me and said that I was a Democrat; then I never said any thing at all; then I came around to the back door of the Court House. When I got around to the back door, Uncle Bill Lanham pointed me out to Mr. Widdicombe, who came to me; he said that he understood that I was going to vote a Democrat ticket; he asked me what ticket was I going to vote; was I going to vote a Democratic ticket. My reply was to him, no, sir; he asked me to let him see my ticket and I showed it to him; he said no, don't you vote that ticket; and when he took my ticket and looked at it and gave it back again, he gave me one of his own tickets and told me that it was the right ticket to vote and not to vote any other; and the reason that I did not vote for Mr. Brooke was because I saw such a great difficulty here that I did not want any body to pull and haul me about; that was the reason that I did not vote for Mr. Brooke. I had tried two doors to get in to vote, but could not get in without difficulty; people were watching me and I could not get in without difficulty at the two back doors. I, after that, went around to the front door and went in and voted a Republican ticket on that account, and after I went in the Court House I had a desire to vote for Mr. Brooke, but there were some men who went in with me at the same time whom I did not care to see me vote, was the reason that I did not vote for him. I was induced to vote the Republican ticket through fear.

Cross-examined:

1st Question.—Did Mr. Widdicombe or any one use any force or violence towards you, and could you not have voted the straight Democratic ticket that Mr. Widdicombe handed back to you if you had desired?

No one used any force or violence towards me. I feared to do it; I was not prevented by force or violence, but I was afraid to do it

2d Question—Did any one prevent you from going into the front door, the usual place of entrance to the polls, where the main body of voters went into vote?

No person prevented me from going into the front door.

3d Question.—Can you read or write, and how do you know you voted the Republican ticket?

I cannot read or write. I know one ticket from another when I see it.

4th Question.—Are you sure you did not make a mistake, and put the Democratic in in place of the Republican ?

No, sir ; I did not make any mistake at all.

5th Question.—Could you not have folded the Democratic ticket up and voted it, and not let any one know it, if you had chosen ?

No, sir ; I do not think I could have done it. There was too many people watching me, and I was afraid to do it.

6th Question.—Would you not have voted the whole Republican ticket if you had been let alone, and but for the interference of Mr. Brooke and Mr. Clagett and others, and did you not vote your real sentiments when you voted the Republican ticket?

No ; I would have voted the whole Democratic ticket if I had been let alone. I did not vote my real sentiments when I voted the Republican ticket.

7th Question.—Were you promised any money or other valuable consideration for voting the Democratic ticket? If so, state by whom and where.

Indeed I wasn't.

8th Question.—What conversation had you with young Mr. Tom Clagett when he took you around the house and looked at your ticket?

I had no conversation, no more than he knew me and called me, and then he asked me if I was going to vote for him. I then took my ticket out of my pocket and showed it to him. He then said that was all right.

9th Question.—Who gave you the ticket you showed to Mr. Clagett, and was it a marked ticket?

Cator Crawford, a colored man who works on Mr. Tom Clagett's place; I do not know whether it was marked or not; he did not tell me he marked it.

10th Question.—Do you understand the nature of an oath, and the consequences of swearing falsely ?

Yes, sir.

11th Question.—Did anybody threaten you after you received the ticket from Crawford, and if so, name him; and if not, why were you frightened and afraid to vote your real sentiments?

Yes, sir; they threatened me so much that they made me stop. Mr. Widdicombe and Uncle Bill Lanham scared me.

12th Question.—Did Mr. Widdicombe threaten you, and if so, what was the nature of the threat?

Yes; he threatened me when he came to me. I knew what it was for at the time he asked me, after he told me that he understood that I was going to vote a Democratic ticket. I then got afraid. He did not threaten my life or anything, and handed the ticket back to me.

13th Question.—What did Uncle Bill Lanham say to you? Did he threaten you?

Did not say anything to me; he only pointed me out to Mr. Widdicombe.

14th Question.—Was there not ample opportunity and time between the opening and closing of the polls on the 4th of November, 1873, for any one wishing to vote to do so, if he chose to remain during the day and wait until the crowd had voted?

I do not know; I could not answer that question, as I did not stay there that long. I know nothing to the contrary.

15th Question.—Do you know of any one who was prevented by force or violence from voting, and who, in consequence of such violence or force, did not vote at the election on the 4th of November, 1873? If yea, give their name or names.

No, sir.

16th Question.—Did you have any conversation with any one before you came here to-day, as to what you should testify to?

[Excepted to by the Contestant as irrelevant.]

No, sir.

17th Question.—You say that you understand the nature and obligations of an oath. State what would be the consequences if you swear falsely.

I do not know, but I will tell as far as I am able. If a man speaks a false oath here, he may expect what will become

of him in the next world. He may expect to be burnt in
hell.

WASHINGTON $\overset{\text{HIS}}{\bowtie}$ JOHNSON.

MARK.

Test: JAMES HARRIS.

Thereupon adjourned until Monday, December 29th, 1873,
at 11 o'clock.

———

DECEMBER 29th, 1873.

Met pursuant to adjournment. No examination, and adjourned until to-morrow, December 30th, 1873.

———

DECEMBER 30th, 1873.

Met pursuant to adjournment.

DEPOSITION No. 20.

CHARLES H. GILL, being duly sworn, deposes as follows:

1st Question.—State your name, age, occupation, place of
residence and where you voted on the 4th day of November,
1873?

My name is Charles H. Hill; age, 31 years; foreman on
the railroad; reside in Upper Marlboro'; I voted in Marlboro',
the Third Election District.

2d Question.—Were you or not deputized by the Sheriff
of this county as special Deputy to guard the polls and to preserve order on the day of election?

I was deputized by Mr. Masters, the Sheriff, to keep order
at the polls that day.

3d Question.—Do you or not know of any interference, by
any officer or other person, with any voter or voters at said
election? If so, state fully all you know about it.

I do; there was a colored man deputized as a special
Deputy Sheriff to preserve order on the day of election, and
he was stationed at the inside door of the Court room, where
the polls were held, and there was only five men allowed to go
into the Judges to vote at one time, and we let those men in
at the front door, and when they got to this other door
they stood for a few minutes, and sometimes for a half
hour when the Judges had any trouble; and while those

men were standing at the door to get in where this colored Deputy was standing, I think his name was Greenleaf, I detected him tearing up tickets; I then watched him and found that he was taking them from the men that were standing at the door going in to vote. I first went and picked up some of the pieces, and found them to be Democratic tickets, by Mr. Brooke's name being upon them. I then went and called Mr. Brooke aside and informed him of it; he went and told the man that he had no right to do it. Mr. Brooke then went away and this man still continued to tear up the tickets; I heard some of the men say that he had no right to see their tickets and refused to show them, and he said that he was stationed there at that door for that purpose—to see all the tickets that went in. I then went and called Mr. Brooke again and told him what was going on, and also Mr. Wedding, a constable of this district. Wr. Wedding told him that he was breaking the law and laid himself liable to be put in jail. I think after that he stopped; when Mr. Wedding went to him about tearing the tickets up, I think I heard him say to Mr. Wedding that he had not torn up more than six or seven.

4th Question.—Do you or not know whether the tickets torn up by this colored Deputy were Democratic tickets and had Mr. Brooke's name upon them?

I do know; I picked the pieces up and examined them; I saw them headed "Democratic Tickets," and saw Mr. Brooke's name on three or four pieces of them.

5th Question.—Did the pieces of tickets seen by you, and torn up by this officer, indicate that there were more than six or seven tickets?

From the pieces under his feet and around him, I am confident that there was not less than six or seven.

6th Question.—Did you or not hear him tell colored voters, as they were approaching the polls, he had a right to examine their tickets?

Yes, I heard him tell them so several times.

7th Question.—Did you or not see colored voters show him their tickets after he stated to them that he was an officer for that purpose?

I did; after they refused to show their tickets, he stated he was stationed there for the purpose of seeing all the tickets that went in the door, and they then showed him their tickets; I can't say that he tore any of these tickets up, I having then gone after Mr. Brooke.

8th Question.—Did or not this colored Deputy have pinned to his breast the badge of office so that all persons could see it?

He had a badge, I think, marked on it "Special Sheriff," pinned on the outside of his coat on his breast, where all could see it.

Cross-examined:

1st Question.—You state in your evidence in chief that a colored man, named Greenleaf, you think, was appointed by the Sheriff, Mr. Masters, Deputy Sheriff, to guard and protect the polls on the day of election, and that the said colored officer took from, and tore up tickets from, colored voters. Do you know whether said colored officer used any threats or violence when taking said tickets, and whether or not he put other tickets in their hands? If so, did you see them vote those tickets, and say whether or not these tickets placed in their hands, if so placed, were Democratic or Republican tickets?

He did not, that I heard; he did put other tickets in their hands; I did not see them vote those tickets; one of them, I am confident, was a Republican ticket, and I did not suppose that he would put one without putting all.

2d Question.—Do you or not know whether these men voted these tickets placed in their hands, willingly or otherwise?

As I stated before, I do not know whether they voted them or not; they did not take them willingly.

3d Question.—Do you know of any Democrats persuading colored Republicans to vote for Mr. Brooke, or whether any inducements were held out to colored voters to vote for Mr. Brooke, and whether you were employed to preserve peace, or to watch Mr. Brooke's interest, and do you know if this colored officer can read or not?

. [The first part of the above question was excepted to by Mr. Brooke as irrelevant.]

I have asked colored voters before the election, and I never heard of any inducements being held out to them to vote for Mr. Brooke. I thought that I was employed for both to keep the peace and see that all went on fair, to keep down riots and rascality; I do not know positively that the colored officer can read or not, but from the manner in which he was handling the tickets, I judged he knew his letters at least.

4th Question.—You state in your evidence in chief that you knew the tickets taken from colored voters by this colored officer were Democratic tickets, because you saw Mr. Brooke's name upon them; don't you know any colored men who voted the Republican ticket with Mr. Brooke's name upon it?

I do not.

5th Question.—If this colored officer violated the law, as you say, why did you not, as a deputized officer, arrest him?

Because Mr. Wedding was there, and he is a higher officer than I was.

6th Question.—Did you see any Democrats tearing up Republican tickets, and if so, did you notify Mr. Widdicombe, and would you have done so?

No, I did not; I dare say I might have, but they never gave me the chance.

7th Question.—Did you or did you not know of any persons entitled to vote, who were prevented by threats, violence, or intimidation, and if there were, was there not ample time for all persons desiring to vote, to do so between the hours of nine A. M. and six P. M. on the election day?

I do not know one. Yes; a man that was not very busy at home could have voted late in the evening.

8th Question.—Do you know of any person or persons voting, whose names were not on the registration list?

ᵥ I do not.

Re-direct by Mr. Brooke:

1st Question.—Did you or did you not suppose that you were appointed to protect Mr. Brooke's interest more than that of any other candidate, Democratic or Republican, and do you know whether Mr. Brooke had anything to do with your appointment, or said anything to you about it or your duties, on that day or previously?

I don't suppose that I was appointed to protect Mr. Brooke's interest any more than any other candidate's. No one said anything to me about whose interest I should protect; it was not the first time that I had been appointed an officer, and I knew a little about the duties of an officer. I do not know whether Mr. Brooke had anything to do with my appointment; he never said anything to me about it or my duties on that day or previously.

C. H. GILL.

Test: JAMES HARRIS.

Thereupon adjourned until half-past nine o'clock A. M., to-morrow.

———

DECEMBER 31st, 1873.

Met pursuant to adjournment.

DEPOSITION No. 21.

WILLIAM B. HILL, being duly sworn, deposes as follows:

1st Question.—State your name, age, occupation, place of residence, and where you voted on the 4th day of November, 1873?

My name is William B. Hill; age, about 60; farmer; reside in Prince George's County, and voted here, the Third Election District.

2d Question.—Was or was not said election, in your opinion, fairly conducted at said polls, and if not, what occurred at the same?

There was a large party of negroes in procession, in ranks, at the polls, filling the door-way, and although I made several efforts to go in, I did not succeed until about twelve o'clock. Of those in ranks I did not recognize other than our colored county men; I saw many strange negroes in the yard; among them was Frank Butler, who formerly belonged to me, and ran away from me before the emancipation, and I had not seen him since that time until the day of election. Those strangers were mixing with the crowd, but can't say that I saw any actual violation of law by them. I saw one of these strange negroes stand near Dr. Sasscer, a little to his side, just after the doctor's trouble in respect to a negro who promised him to vote the Democratic ticket and did not do so, and while the doctor was recounting to myself and others the circumstances of the case, this negro stood by with both fists doubled, seeking evidently to provoke a quarrel; I did not attract the doctor's attention to it, because I thought it might give the negro the opportunity to get the difficulty that he was seeking.

Cross-examined:

1st Question.—Was there not ample opportunity and time between the opening and closing of the polls on the 4th day of November, 1873, at the Third Election District, for any one wishing to vote to do so, if he chose to wait until the crowd had voted?

I believe there was.

2d Question.—Do you know of any one who was prevented by violence or intimidation from voting at said election ; if so, please name him?

I know one, named John Owens, who was in my service, and who had promised some persons at the Landing to vote the Democratic ticket. I understood he did not come here that day, and gave as a reason that he heard that there was fighting here and did not come. I know of no other.

WM. B. HILL.

Test : JAMES HARRIS.

Thereupon adjourned until 10 o'clock A. M., to-morrow morning.

JANUARY 1st, 1874.

Met pursuant to adjournment.

There being no witnesses in attendance, adjourned until 10 A. M., to-morrow morning.

JANUARY 2d, 1874.

Met pursuant to adjournment.

DEPOSITION No. 22.

JAMES MULLIKIN, being duly sworn, deposed as follows :

1st Question.—State your name, age, occupation, place of residence, and where you voted on the 4th day of November, 1873.

My name is James Mullikin ; age, 59 ; farmer ; residence, in Queen Anne District, Prince George's County, where I voted on the 4th day of November, 1873.

2d Question.—Do you or do you not know of any interference by parties with any voter or voters at said election, and of any intimidation of voters at the same ; if yea, state all you know about it?

I was Judge that day of election ; there was a colored man came in to vote, when, just as he was handing me his ticket to put in the ballot-box, James Parker said that he must see the ticket before it was voted. I am not sure, but think Mr. Solomon Chaney came up at the time with several others, but I can't recollect their names. I told them that they must leave the room ; that they could not have their fuss there ; that they were preventing the election from going on. They took the man and went off. I did not see any intimidation. I was acting as Judge and did not leave my seat during the day except to get my dinner. There were only two Judges present ; the Republican Judge did not attend. I heard it said that they were fighting outside. I did not see any fighting myself.

Cross-examined :

1st Question.—Was the ticket handed you by the colored man himself, and did you have it in your hands ; what was his name, and did he make any remarks, and can you say positively whether he had a Democratic or Republican ticket ; whether James Parker used any force or violence, or threatened him in any manner ?

The ticket was handed me by the colored man himself ; I was in the act of taking it, and had my hand on it, when the interference took place, when I immediately let it go. Some one said why don't you put it in the box. The colored man said that was the ticket he wanted to vote, but he still held on to the ticket. I could only tell what kind of ticket it was by feeling the paper ; the ticket was folded. James Parker used no force or violence, only said that he wanted to see that ticket. I then ordered them to quit the room and they left. I do not know the parties' names. He voted afterwards during the day. I don't know how he voted. He came back with the same parties he left, and I think he had the same ticket he first offered.

2d Question.—Do you know of any Democratic tickets having been voted on the said day of election, marked "True Blue," and was not your attention called to the fact that there was a ticket marked "True Blue ;" the marked used by Judge Peach, when you were taking the tickets out of the ballot-box ?

There was one, marked "True Blue," came out of the ballot-box.

3d Question.—Was there not ample opportunity and time between the opening and closing of the polls on the 4th day of November, 1873, for any one wishing to vote to do so, if he chose to remain during the day and wait until the crowd voted?

There was.

4th Question.—Do you know of any one who was prevented by violence or force from voting, and who, in consequence of such violence or force, did not vote at said election on the 4th of November, 1873? If yea, give their name or names.

I know of no one that day. There was no interference at the polls on that day, except the one I mentioned previously.

5th Question.—Do you know of any one who voted at said election in your district, or elsewhere in the county, who had not been registered?

I do not know of any.

6th Question.—Do you know of any colored men who were brought in at the back door by Democrats in a drunken state, and voted the Democratic ticket? If yea, give their name or names.

I do not know.

7th Question.—Do you know of any colored men who were solicited to vote the Democratic ticket, or who voted said ticket of their own account?

I know several who told me, of their own accord, that they were going to vote the Democratic ticket. They voted; can't say how they voted.

8th Question.—You state that yourself and Judge Peach, in the absence of the Republican Judge, conducted the said election, and that nothing unusual or different occurred at said election from what occurs at elections ordinarily, and that the said election was conducted fairly, and in accordance with law.

It was.

Recalled by Mr. Brooke:

1st Question.—Do you or not know of any colored men's names being put upon the registration books on the day of election, and if yea, state how many names were so put on, and whether the parties voted or not?

There were some colored men's names put on the registra-

5

tion book on the day of election by the Registrar. I do not recollect how many, nor their names, but they all voted.

2d Question.—Did you or not see any voter or voters the day after said election, who told you that he or they were prevented from voting the Democratic ticket on said day of election, by intimidation? If yea, give the names of said parties, and state all they said on the subject.

I did see one. I went to the postoffice to get my mail, and on my return home I passed a negro man by the name of Jacob Oakey. He asked me if I would stop awhile, that he wanted to speak to me. He said to me that "I did not vote yesterday." I told him I knew he had not, and asked him why. He said he wanted to vote the Democratic ticket, and, taking the ticket out of his pocket, said, "Here is my ticket." I told him that I did not want the ticket, and asked him why he did not vote the ticket at the ballot-box. He said that he was afraid to do it; they threatened to kill him if he voted that ticket. I asked him who threatened him; he said the Republican party. I then asked him to tell me who did it; that I would see him righted. He said he was afraid to do that; he was afraid to tell me who. This is all. I told him that I had not time to stand and talk with him; that the election was over.

Re-cross-examined :

1st Question.—You were one of the Democratic Judges on the day of election. State whether or not the names of white and colored voters referred to by you were not put on the poll book at your instance and by your direction, because their names had been left off inadvertently by the Registrar, who was present, and admitted that they had been so left off, and that the parties referred to were known by yourself and the Registrar to be legally qualified voters, and state if you know how they voted.

I was one of the Democratic Judges at said election. The names of the white and colored voters referred to were put on the poll book at my request, because I knew that they were entitled to vote, and that the Registrar had made some mistake in transferring their names from one book to the other. I do not know how they voted.

2d Question.—You were at the window all day. Did you

see the party, Jacob Oakey, offer to vote, and did you see any intimidation used to prevent him from voting?

I don't recollect of seeing him at all.

JAMES MULLIKIN.

Test: JAMES HARRIS.

DEPOSITION No. 23.

JOHN W. BELT (Oak Grove), being duly sworn, deposes as follows:

1st Question.—State your name, age, occupation, place of residence, and where you voted on the 4th day of November, 1873.

My name is John W. Belt; 28 years old; merchant, Oak Grove, and voted in the Third Election District of Prince George's County.

2d Question.—Do you or not know of any minor who voted at said polls on said day of election? If yea, state fully all you know about it.

I can't say whether he was a minor or not, but there was a boy that voted here by the name of Henry Holland; I do not know his age. After the election, I was talking about it one night at the store and the boy was on the counter; I happened to remark that it was a pity for the boy to be misled if he was under age; he replied that it was not his fault. I said nothing more to him about it; he seemed to be distressed about it.

3d Question.—Have you or not had any conversation with Charles C. Hill as to Henry Holland, since the election, and his voting? If so, state what that conversation was?

I have; I remarked one day to Mr. Hill about this boy's voting; his reply was that he was not of age, and, as well as I can remember, his reply was that he was not twenty years of age.

4th Question.—Do you or not know of any interference by any candidates or other parties with any voter or voters at said election? If yea, state all you know about it.

I know that Mr. Widdicombe was looking at the tickets of voters before they could get to the box to deposit their ballots, and I saw that it had a tendency to prevent men from voting their sentiments, and I remonstrated and asked him, Mr. Widdicombe, if he thought that was exactly fair ; his reply was, if I did not believe that every colored man would vote a ticket headed Republican or a Republican ticket if let alone ? My reply was that I did not think so if they knew who they were voting for ; that I did not consider that there was more than three Republicans on the ticket ; that they were all Democrats, and that I thought people ought to vote for the best man. A colored man came to vote, named Henry Sprigg ; Mr. Widdicombe held out his hand and the boy handed him his ticket ; I asked him if he had voted ; he said, yes, and started out and said that gentleman, pointing to Mr. Widdicombe, had his ticket ; I told him that he had not voted—that his ticket would have to go into that box, pointing to the ballot-box ; I gave him another ticket, and, before he could vote, Mr. Widdicombe came up and took the ticket from him and told him here was his ticket ; I then asked him if he knew how he voted ; he replied that he voted the Democratic ticket ; I told him that he had not, and showed him the ticket that Mr. Widdicombe took from him, which I picked from the floor where Mr. Widdicombe threw it. A short time after Henry Sprigg, Sr., the father of the said Henry Sprigg, came in, and I asked him if he had his ticket ; he said he had ; I told him that his son, Henry, had been fooled out of his vote ; he got very indignant about it and went out and brought Mr. Charles Hill in ; Mr. Hill and Mr. Widdicombe had a talk about the affair ; I do not know what the conversation was.

5th Question.—Had Henry Sprigg, Jr., promised you, prior to voting, to vote the Democratic ticket?

He told me that he intended to vote the Democratic ticket ; I don't think I asked him anything about it ; he told me voluntarily.

6th Question.—How near was Mr. Widdicombe to the ballot-box when this ticket was taken from Henry Sprigg, Jr. ?

I can't say exactly, but think it was about three or four feet.

7th Question.—Did or not any voter or voters tell you after the election was over that they had been prevented from voting as they wished, by intimidation or otherwise ? If yea, state who, what they said and all you know about it?

They did ; James Shorter met me at Oak Grove the night of the election and said that he wanted to vote the Democratic ticket, but, my God ! Mr. Belt, I could not let those men kill me ; I asked him who they were ; he said that he did not know their names, but thought it was some of those Washington boys.   Abram Coats said he intended to vote the Democratic ticket, but the men said what they would do to him in case he did.

Cross-examined :

1st *Question.*—Do you know of any colored man or men who voted the Democratic ticket?   If so, name him or them.

Henry Sprigg, Sr., Charles Giles and a number of others.

2d *Question.*—Do you know any colored man or men who were taken by the back door to the polls whilst under the influence of liquor, and if they succeeded in voting the Democratic ticket without molestation or intimidation ?

I do not know of any.

3d *Question.*—Did you see Henry Holland vote, and are you positive he voted the Republican ticket ?

I saw him vote ; did not see the ticket.

4th *Question.*—Did you ask any colored man on the day of election to show his ticket, and is it not customary for both parties to ask to see tickets at the polls and use all their influence to procure votes legitimately ?

I do not recollect of asking any man at the polls to show me his ticket ; I may have asked them if they had had their tickets taken away and another given in their place.   I can't say anything about the custom ; I never saw such actions at the polls since I have been a voter.

5th *Question.*—Did you not see Democrats, on said day of election, doing their utmost to get colored men to vote the Democratic ticket, and did you not, before and on the day of election, use your influence to secure as many colored votes as possible for Mr. Brooke, and in pursuance of that object did you not bring down a wagon-load of colored voters, who voted for Mr. Brooke ?

I saw some Democrats talking to colored men on the day of election, but can't say what they were talking about.   I did use my influence for the whole Democratic ticket, before the election, but not until I had explained to those who were supposed not to know the men on both tickets, and asked them to vote for the best men ; that I thought the Democratic party had the best men in the field. I brought two wagon-loads of voters, white and colored ; they had the Democratic tickets, and said they voted them.

6th Question.—Did you not think Mr. Widdicombe had the same right to endeavor to secure votes and to ask to see a colored man's ticket, and to give him a ticket, if a party asked for it, as any Democrat had?

Yes.

7th Question.—Did not Mr. Wddicombe say to you that he believed in every one voting as he wished?

I don't recollect of Mr. Widdicombe saying that ; but as I said before, Mr. Widdicombe asked me if I did not think the colored people would not vote the Republican ticket, if no one said anything to them?

8th Question.—Do you know whether it was a Democratic or Republican ticket that the man Sprigg handed to Widdicombe, and did not Mr. Widdicombe give back the same ticket that he took from him, and was not the ticket picked up by you, thrown down by the colored man, and not by Mr. Widdicombe?

I do not know whether it was the same ticket ; I know that Mr. Widdicombe gave him a Republican ticket, which the man Sprigg voted ; do not know whether the man threw the ticket down, or Mr. Widdicombe.

9th Question.—How do you know it was a Republican ticket, and if it was, how do you know whether or not Mr. Brooke's name was upon it?

I saw the ticket ; I do not know whether Mr. Brooke's name was on it or not.

10th Question.—How do you know that the parties referred to in your examination-in-chief as having been prevented from voting by intimidation, had offered to vote, or had been refused by the Judges of Election ?

I saw them both vote ; I saw one of them vote the Republican ticket ; the other said at the polls that he was going to vote the Republican ticket.

11th Question.—Has it not been dangerous for colored men around you to admit that they voted the Republican ticket, and did you not have a difficulty with a colored man for voting the Republican ticket?

No, sir ; the man that I had the difficulty with claimed to have voted the Democratic ticket.

12th Question.—What time of the day was it when you left your store on the morning of the election, and was not a majority of the men brought down by you in a wagon, in a beastly state of intoxication from whisky, given to them by you, or at your store?

No, sir.

13th Question.—Do not you think it likely that the man Shorter, who told you, at your store, after the election, that he was afraid to vote, made the remark in jest, and in order to get a drink of whisky, and do you know whether he voted or not, and how he voted?

No ; I do not think he did. He voted, and voted the Republican ticket.

14th Question.—Was there not ample opportunity and time between the opening and the closing of the polls, on the 4th of November, 1873, for any one wishing to vote to do so, if he chose to remain during the day and wait until the crowd had voted?

Yes.

15th Question.—Do you know of any one who was prevented, by violence or force, from voting, and who, in consequence of such violence, or force, did not vote at the election held on the 4th of November, 1873 ; if yea, give name or names.

I do not know of any one who did not vote. I do not know of any one who voted who had not been registered.

16th Question.—In your examination-in-chief you stated that Mr. Widdicombe took tickets from voters and gave them others in their stead. Please state the exact number taken, and whether or not he used any force or threats towards these parties, and the name of the parties.

It would be impossible for me to state the number. I did not hear Mr. Widdicombe use any threats or use any violence. I can't name the parties from whom he took the tickets.

Test : JAMES HARRIS.   JNO. W. BELT.

Thereupon adjourned until to-morrow morning, 9½ o'clock.

JANUARY 3d, 1874.

Met pursuant to adjournment. There being no witness in attendance, adjourned until Monday, January 5th, 1874, at 10 o'clock, A. M.

JANUARY 5th, 1874.

Met pursuant to adjournment.

DEPOSITION NO. 24.

ROBERT N. PUMPHREY, being duly sworn, deposes as follows:

1st Question.—State your name, age, occupation, place of residence, and where you voted on the 4th November, 1873.

My name is Robert H. Pumphrey; aged 29; occupation, farmer; reside in Prince George's County, and vote at Upper Marlboro'.

2d Question.—Do you or do you not know of any interference of parties with any voter or voters at said election? If yea, state all you know about it.

Certainly; I brought down a negro man, Alec Gross, who said that he wanted to vote the Democratic ticket, and when getting out, he was taken by his son, Alec Gross, Jr., and asked how he was going to vote. He said that he wanted to vote the Democratic ticket, and his son Alec then caught hold of him and pulled him down on the ground, and the crowd trampled on him and disabled him so that he was unable to work for a day or two. He did not vote. On his return home I asked him whether he voted or not, and he said he did not, that he was afraid. The crowd made no threats, but rushed in. I told them to stand off; that he wanted to vote the Democratic ticket. His son Alec then said he should not, and took him off.

Cross-examined:

1st Question.—Where and when did this man, Alec, tell you he wanted to vote, and had you asked him to vote the Democratic ticket, and did you attempt to influence him by promises or threats, and is he in your employ?

He told me at home on the morning of the election, and also down here. I did not ask him to vote the Democratic ticket. I did not attempt to influence him. I went down on the morning of the election, and asked him whether he wanted to vote, and his reply was that I had been his best friend and he wanted to vote as I did. I told him that I intended to vote the Democratic ticket, and he then said that was the ticket he wanted to vote. He was in my employ.

2d Question.—Did not the old man fall when his son pulled him because he was very drunk, and was not the trampling accidental, because of his having fallen at the time of the contest for his vote between you and his son?

No, sir; he was not drunk. I don't think that he had had a drink that day. I don't think it was accidental; I hardly know what to call it: would not like to say that it was or was not. The crowd had gotten him some distance from me when they pulled him down and trampled over him. I presume it was done to prevent my getting to him.

3d Question.—When his son said that he should not vote the Democratic ticket, and asked him to go with him, did he refuse to go and try to remain with you?

His son did not ask him any questions, but took him by violence by the arm and carried him off. This was after he had told him that he should not vote the Democratic ticket.

4th Question.—Did you not resist very vigorously, and strike several blows before you were struck, or were you struck accidentally?

I did not resist very vigorously, but told his son that he should vote the way he wanted to vote. I think from the awkward manner in which I was struck that it was an accident.

5th Question.—How do you know that the old man Alec did not vote the Democratic ticket, and did not Mr. William B. Bowie take him up and vote him?

I know only what he told me, which was that he did not vote at all.

6th Question.—Were you not made a deputy to look after Mr. Brooke's interest and to see that parties voted the Democratic ticket, and would you have brought the old man down if he had wanted to vote the Republican ticket?

No, sir. I was not. I don't know whether he would have brought him down or not.

7th Question.—Was there not ample opportunity and time between the opening and the closing of the poll on the 4th day of November, 1873, for any one wishing to vote to do so, if he chose to remain during the day and wait until the crowd had voted?

I suppose so. I did not remain all day.

8th Question.—Do you know of any one who voted at said election in your district or elsewhere in the county, who had not been registered?

I do not.

ROBERT H. PUMPHREY.

Test : James Harris.

Deposition No. 25.

Enos F. Pumphrey, being first duly sworn, deposes as follows :

1st Question.—State your name, age, occupation, place of residence and where you voted on the 4th day of November, 1873?

My name is Enos F. Pumphrey ; age, 30 years ; farmer, and I voted in Marlboro'.

2d Question.—Do you or not know of any interference by parties with any voter or voters at said election? If yea, state all you know about it.

There was an old man, Alec he is called ; I don't know his other name ; was on his way to the Court House to vote ; he was at the Court House gate entrance, when he was seized by a parcel of men and taken back into the street, and they said that he should not vote the Democratic ticket ; they took him from the back entrance and carried him around in front of the Court House. They dragged him. I could not tell how many there were ; there were a large crowd of them ; I followed through the yard and met them at the front gate and went in amongst them and tried to break him away from them, but did not succeed, for as fast as one let go, another would catch hold, and I did not succeed in getting him entirely clear of them until opposite to Mr. Turner's. I then asked him who he wanted to vote for ; he said that he wanted to vote for Mr. Brooke and Mr. Clarke ; that those were all that he wanted to vote for. Some three or four of that crowd then said that the y would be damned if he should. The old man then said that he had been hauled and dragged and was completely be-wildered. I then told the old man that he should vote for whom he wanted. I started with the old man, but the crowd kept in front crowding on so that I could not get in the gate. The old man then said that he would not vote at all ; that he had been pulled and hauled and all his clothes torn off; that he would not get over it for two or three years. Some of them said that it was a good thing that your clothes were torn off ; you shan't go in there to vote. I asked them if they were trying to raise a disturbance, or trying to intimidate him and keep him from voting. They then began to curse and swear, as if they were trying to raise a fuss sure enough, and making remarks which I do not recollect. I remarked to them that the first one that raised a fuss I would arrest him and put him in jail, if I had to deputize all on the ground to do so. Alec then went off and did not vote at all. I think I did not see him again that day.

Cross-examined.

1st Question.—How do you know how this old man, Alec, wanted to vote, and had he told you that he wanted to vote the Democratic ticket before you took him from the crowd, and was it not a contest between both parties to get his vote, and did not the Democrats finally succeed in getting posses-sion of him ?

I did not know how he wanted to vote; he had not told me ; all that I saw around him were colored men when I got him away ; I do not know to what party they belonged, except some of them saying that he should not vote the Democratic ticket. I was a Deputy Sheriff and finally got him out of the crowd.

2d Question.—Was not your rushing into the crowd to take possession of the old man calculated to create a disturbance and injury, and was not the disturbance, if any, the result of your conduct?

No, sir.

3d Question.—Did you or not see Mr. William B. Bowie take this old man, Alec, from the crowd and carry him up to the polls by the back way?

I did not ; I did not see him vote at all.

4th Question.—Was it not considered that the Democrats

had a little the advantage of the Republicans in the back door voting?

I do not know whether they had or not.

. *5th Question.*—Was there not ample opportunity. and time between the opening and closing of the polls on the 4th of November, 1873, for any one wishing to vote to do so, if he chose to remain during the day and wait until the crowd had voted?

I suppose there was.

6th Question.—Do you know of any one who was prevented by violence or force from voting, and who, in consequence of such violence or force, did not vote at the election held on the 4th of November, 1873? If yea, give name or names.

I do not know of any.

ENOS F. PUMPHREY.

Test: JAMES HARRIS.

DEPOSITION NO. 26.

WILLIAM P. PUMPHREY, being duly sworn, deposes as follows:

1st Question.—State your name, age, occupation, place of residence, and where you voted on the 4th of November, 1873.

My name is William P. Pumphrey; age, 60 years; occupation, farmer; in Marlboro' District, Prince George's County, where I voted on the 4th of November, 1873.

2d Question.—Do you or do you not know of any intimidation used to prevent any person or persons from voting the Democratic ticket at the election held on said day? If yea, give their name or names and state all you know about it.

I only know in the case of this old man, Alec Gross; I was coming in Marlboro', between the hours of eleven and twelve o'clock; I met the old man at William Harper's drug store, and asked him if he had voted; he looked very bad, his face covered with sand; he said no, that he was prevented from voting by being pulled and hauled and was very much crippled; I asked him to go back with me and go in with me and vote; he replied that "he was afraid, and don't you go up, Massa Williams; I am afraid that both of us will be killed." He seemed to be very much frightened; he went into Mr. Wilson's store; I came to the Court House and got George Wilson, Jr., to go down with me to the store and try to get him

to come up to vote; when we got there he was gone; the
next morning I said, "why, Alec, you are a pretty fellow to get
scared." He said it was enough to scare him ; he told me that
he had his ticket in his pocket, and he was not able to work
for several days, during which time I visited him every day
at his quarter ; he worked on my farm and is still there.

WM. P. PUMPHREY.

Test : JAMES HARRIS.

Before Mr. Pumphrey was sworn he was objected to, on the
ground that his name does not appear upon either of the notices served upon Mr. Robert S. Widdicombe or his attorney.

DEPOSITION No. 26.

BENJAMIN F. GUY, being first duly sworn, deposes as follows :

1st Question.—State your name, age, occupation, place of
residence and where you voted on the 4th day of November,
1873. ?

My name is Benjamin F. Guy; age, 43; occupation, merchant; reside in Hyattsville, Prince George's County, and
voted at Bladensburg.

2d Question.—Do you or do you not know of any non-residents of the county or State who voted with the Republican
party at said election? And if yea, how long have each of
said parties removed from the county, and where do they now
reside?

I do not know whether I do or not ; Mr. George Jackson I
do regard as a non-resident, who, to the best of my knowledge,
has been out of the county for two years prior to the election ;
I can't say positively where he resides ; my impression is that
he resides in Washington ; I do not know whether he voted
or not.

Cross-examined :

1st Question.—Do you know whether George W. Jackson
has been registered or not, and whether his name appeared on
the poll-book furnished by the Registrar to the Judges of
Election, and do you know of your own knowledge that he
voted and how he voted? And if you know he voted at any
other place, and whether his letters are not mailed to his address at Hyattsville, and if he left with the intention of residing permanently elsewhere?

I do not know whether he has been registered or not ; I have not examined the poll-books, and do not know whether his name is there or not. I do not know that he voted ; I do not know that he ever voted elsewhere. He has papers addressed to him from Marlboro' regularly ; I can't say that there has been any letters for him ; the papers are taken out of the office by his brother. I could not possibly say what his intentions were. He was elected County Surveyor at last election.

2d Question.—Was there not ample opportunity and time, between the opening and closing of the polls, at Bladensburg, on the 4th of November, 1873, for any one wishing to vote to do so, if he chose to remain during the day, and wait until the crowd had voted?

I can't say positively, because I was not at the polls all day ; I know nothing to the contrary.

3d Question.—Do you know of any one who was prevented, by violence or force,.from voting, and who, in consequence of such violence or force, did not vote at the election held on the 4th of November, 1873 ; if yea, give name or names?

I do not.

4th Question.—Do you know of any one who voted at said election, in your district or elsewhere in the county, who had not been registered?

I do not.

B. F. GUY.

Test : JAMES HARRIS.

DEPOSITION No. 27.

J. R. H. DEAKINS, being duly sworn, deposes as follows :

1st Question.—State your name, age, occupation, place of residence, and where you voted on the 4th day of November, 1873.

My name is J. R. H. Deakins ; age, 31 years ; occupation, farmer ; reside near Bladensburg. I did not vote on the 4th of November, 1873 ; was not in the State at that time.

2d Question.—Do you or not know Mr. Frederick Fowke, and if so, state if he has ever resided in this county, and for what period of time?

I know him slightly ; do not know positively that he ever

resided in this county. Last winter he staid at Mr. Thomas
Jackson's, and at his sister's awhile; how long, I do not
know; he came there from Virginia. He voted at the last
election, as shown by the Registrar's poll-books, in Bladensburg District. I have examined the poll and registration
books since I came here. He came in the county a little over
a year ago, but it is my impression that he has passed the
majority of his time in Washington.

Cross-examined.

1st Question.—Do you know Frederick Fowke; has he or
has he not resided long enough in Bladensburg District to
entitle him to be registered and to vote, and how do you
know it?

I do not know if he has resided long enough in Bladensburg District to entitle him to be registered and to vote, and
do not know how he voted.

J. R. H. DEAKINS.

Test: JAMES HARRIS.

DEPOSITION No. 28.

JOHN B. BROOKE, being duly sworn, deposes as follows:

1st Question.—State your name, age, occupation, place of
residence, and where you voted on the 4th of November, 1873?

My name is John B. Brooke; age, 46; occupation, lawyer;
my place of residence is in Prince George's County; I voted
in Upper Marlboro'.

2d Question.—Do you or do you not know of any non-residents of the county or State, who voted with the Republican
party at said election; if yea, state how long since said parties
removed from the county, and where they now reside?

I assume that this question has been asked with regard to
my brothers, Albert and Eugene Brooke. I do not know how
they voted, but I know they claim to be voting with the Republican party; I should judge from their political associa-
tions that they did so. I think, as well as I can recollect,
that Eugene went to Washington in the fall of 1869, and
went into business there in the spring of 1870. Albert, to
the best of my knowledge, never had any home since in his
mother's house, except that he was in the employ of Mr.
Henry Brooke, in the Clerk's Office, for six months or longer.

I never knew him to have any occupation in the county, except at that time. He went to Washington on the 1st of January, 1870, when his mother gave up possession of her farm and went there to reside. I can't speak of their political residence, but if anybody had asked me where either of them lived, who wished to see them on business or for any other purpose, I should have said in Washington City, up to the date of the election. Albert is still in Washington, and Eugene has been on a visit to me for several weeks.

Cross-examined:

1st Question.—How long after your mother removed to Washington was it before she had a home of her own?

I think, to the best of my recollection, that she had a home of her own since the fall of 1872.

2d Question.—Do you know where Albert and Eugene Brooke have been voting for the last several years, where they claimed their residence, and whether their removal to Washington was permanent or not?

I never saw Albert or Eugene deposit a ballot in my life, but I know that they have come to these polls since 1869 for the purpose of voting. They both told me so, and to the best of my knowledge and belief they have both been voting here since 1869, up to the day of the election. I have never heard them say where they claimed their residence. I do not know that their removal to Washington was permanent or not.

3d Question.—Do you not know that they have been sojourning on business temporarily in St. Mary's County for several months during the last year?

Nothing, except what I heard from them; they both told me that they had.

4th Question.—Do you know of any one, and if so name him, who was prevented by violence or intimidation from voting on the 4th of November last, in Prince George's County?

I do not.

5th Question.—Was there not ample opportunity and time between the opening and closing of the polls on the 4th of November, 1873, in the Third Election District, or Marlboro' District, for any one wishing to vote to do so, if he chose to remain and wait?

I was not here at the opening of the polls. I saw no difficulty in voting, provided you had a little patience. I arrived at 11 o'clock, and voted between 3 and 4 o'clock. There was no difficulty when I voted; if there had been any difficulty, I was not a witness to it.

JNO. B. BROOKE.

Test: JAMES HARRIS.

DEPOSITION No. 29.

JUDSON F. RICHARDSON, being duly sworn, deposes as follows:

1st Question.—State your name, age, occupation, place of residence, and where you voted on the 4th day of November, 1873.

My name is Judson F. Richardson; age, 52; occupation, hotel-keeper; reside in Prince George's County, and voted at Bladensburg.

2d Question.—Do you or do you not know of any non-residents of the county or State who voted with the Republican party at said election? If yea, give their names, state how long since they removed from the county, and where they now reside.

I know one fellow, who lives in Washington and voted at Bladensburg. I guess he voted with the Republican party. He had a No. 3 ticket. He was living in Washington when I moved to Bladensburg, and that has been nearly three years. He still lives there. His name is Joseph H. Beall. I never knew that there was an H in his name until I saw it on the poll-book to-day at the Clerk's office.

Cross-examined:

1st Question.—Do you know whether Joseph H. Beall was registered, and whether his name appeared on the poll-book on the day of election, and do you know, of your own knowledge, that he voted the Republican ticket, and might not a Democratic ticket have contained the number 3?

Yes; I saw it there. I know he voted the Republican ticket, because I saw it.

2d Question.—Do you know whether he has voted anywhere else since you say he left the county, and if, to your knowledge, he left the county to reside permanently elsewhere?

6

I never saw him vote; he never told me that he had left the county permanently.

3d Question.—Do you know of any other parties who voted the Democratic ticket, who have been out of the county as long as he has?

I do not.

4th Question.—Do you not know parties voting a Republican ticket with the names of Democratic candidates upon it, and parties voting the Democratic ticket with Republican names on it, and might not this ticket, marked No. 3, which you say was voted by Beall, been one of that character?

I know a party with a Republican ticket with Democratic names on it, who came up to vote, and it was snatched out of his hand by Mr. Danenhower and torn up. Yes; I put Mr. Wallis' name on about sixty myself. I don't think it was; I saw nearly every name on it.

5th Question.—Did the man referred to, by you, object to Mr. Danenhower tearing his ticket, and did he not take another ticket offered by Mr. D., and was that the only ticket taken away from parties that day and torn up?

I do not think he had time to object, but he went to Dr. Wells and asked him to make him out another ticket exactly like it, and went up and voted. The ticket torn up was a Republican ticket with two Democratic names upon it. It was the only ticket I saw taken away and torn up that day.

6th Question.—Was there not ample opportunity and time between the opening and closing of the polls at Bladensburg, on the 4th of November, 1873, for any one wishing to vote to do so, if he chose to remain during the day and wait until the crowd had voted?

There was.

7th Question.—Do you know of any one who was prevented by violence or force from voting, and who, in consequence of such violence or force, did not vote at the election held on the 4th of November, 1873? If yea, give name or names.

There was a party that went up with Dr. Wells to vote, who was taken away by Plummer and others, and carried off up the street, and afterwards came with Plummer and voted, I think. That is the only case I know of.

8th Question.—Do you know of any one who voted at said

election in your district or elsewhere in the county, who had not been registered?

I do not.

Re-called by Mr. Brooke:

1st Question.—Do you or not know of any party duly registered who was not permitted to vote at said election?

I do. John Hays. There was a Republican, who was also registered, but did not vote because his name could not be found, but was afterwards found and he was sent for, but he had left.

Re-cross-examined:

1st Question.—Do you know if John Hays, who offered to vote, was refused by the Judges, and why they refused to take his vote?

Because they could not find his name on the poll-book. He has been a voter there for eight or ten years.

JUDSON F. RICHARDSON.

Test: JAMES HARRIS.

Thereupon adjourned until to-morrow morning at 9½ o'clock.

————

JANUARY 6th, 1874.

Met pursuant to adjournment.

DEPOSITION No. 30.

J. L. JARBOE, having been duly sworn, deposes as follows:

1st Question.—State your name, age, occupation, place of residence and where you voted on the 4th day of November, 1873?

My name is Joseph L. Jarboe; age, 25; occupation, clerk; reside in Marlboro', and voted in the Ninth (Surratt's) District, Prince George's County.

2d Question.—Do you or do you not know of any interference, by candidates or other parties, with any voter or voters on the day of said election? If yea, state fully all about it.

I do, sir. Mr. A. V. Robey carried a man away from Mr. Hutchinson's house, about 2 o'clock or later, on the morning of the election. As I was coming out of Hutchinson's door I saw one man pulling another; I asked what was the matter,

and some one remarked that Jenkins was trying to carry this
man away ; I told Jenkins that he could not carry him away
unless he wanted to go ; I then told him to let the man go ;
he did so ; and the man went back into the house with me.
I then went out of the house, but left the man in the house.
A short time afterwards, I saw several men coming from towards the house ; they seemed to be pulling some one with
them.   I went up to see who it was and I found that it was
the same man that I had taken from Jenkins, and before I
could get this man from them, they threw him into Robey's
buggy, and Robey jumped in and started with him.   I stopped
Mr. Robey's horse, and told Mr. Robey that that man did not
want to go and that he could not carry him away from there ;
he tried to get away the best he could, but I held his horse ;
a great many persons gathered around and made so much
noise that I could scarcely hear what was going on.   I told
them that if they would keep quiet a moment, and if the man
said that he wanted to go, he could go.   During that, Robey
was trying to get away all the time.   I then asked the man
if he wanted to go ; he said he would go, but would come
back and vote with me in the morning.   I then let Robey pass.

Cross-examined :

1st Question.—Do you know whether the party went away
with Mr. Robey without resistance ; whether or not he had not
privately requested Mr. Robey to take him away because of the
interference of the Democrats, who wanted him to vote against
his wishes ?

He went away with Mr. Robey ; I don't think he tried to
get out of the buggy ; I don't think any Democrats asked him
to vote against his wishes.

2d Question.—Was not this meeting at Hutchinson's, the
night before the election, held for the purpose of influencing
any colored voters to vote the Democratic ticket, and was that
not an interference with the election, if the other was ?

I don't think it was ; there were a good many colored persons there, and I believe they would have voted the ticket if
they had not been carried away ; it was not an interference
with the election ; this man, whose name I do not know, was
carried away from the house by force ; he said he was a voter.

3d Question.—Do you know or not whether this party,

whose name you do not know, was going away with Mr. Jenkins, the party who first had him in charge, and from whom you took him, on business or political mission?

I presume he was taking him away to make him vote the Republican ticket.

4th Question.—Did the party or parties who were taking the man away avow that it was their purpose of voting him the next day against his wishes, and did he claim your protection against them?

They did not say that they intended to vote him; he did not ask my protection, but I thought he needed it.

5th Question.—Do you know whether this man who went away with Mr. Robey voted the next day or not, and how he voted?

I do not know whether he voted or how he voted.

6th Question.—Was there not ample opportunity and time, between the opening and closing of the polls on the 4th of November, 1873, at your election polls, for any one wishing to vote to do so, if he chose to remain and wait until the crowd had voted?

Yes, sir.

7th Question.—Do you know of any one who was prevented by violence or force from voting, and who, in consequence of such violence or force, did not vote at the election held in your district on the 4th of November, 1873? If yea, give name or names.

I do not.

8th Question.—Do you know of any one who voted at your district or elsewhere in the county, who had not been registered?

I do not.

Re-called by Mr. Brooke:

1st Question.—Do you or do you not know of any attempt to influence the colored voters on said day of election?

I heard John Simms say on the day of election, whilst the voting was going on, near the window where the ballots were received, that no colored man had better vote the Democratic ticket; some one asked him why, and he said that "I will go for him."

Re-cross-examined:

1st Question.—Do you know whether any voter was pre-

vented from voting by the remarks made by John Simms?
If yea, give name or names.

I can't say whether any one was prevented from voting, but
I think the remark was calculated to intimidate those that
were standing around.

J. L. JARBOE.

Test : JAMES HARRIS.

DEPOSITION No. 31.

C. C. MAGRUDER, JR., being duly sworn, deposes as follows :

1st Question.—State your name, age, occupation, place of
residence, and where you voted on the 4th of November, 1873.

My name is C. C. Magruder, Jr. ; age, 34 years ; occupation,
attorney at law ; reside in Upper Marlboro', Prince George's
County, Maryland, where I voted at the election held on the
4th of November, 1873.

2d Question.—Do you or do you not know of any interference by parties with any voter or voters, on the day of said
election, or of any intimidation or violence used to prevent
parties from voting the Democratic ticket ?

I was standing in the Court House yard on the morning of
the election, and saw a wagon driven by the Court House, on
the side next to Gardner's Hotel, by one of the young Mr.
Pumphreys. I do not know his name. There were two or
three white and five or six colored men in it. I went around
on the eastern side of the Hall building, where the wagon
had stopped, and the parties alighted therefrom. Among the
number who got out of the wagon was Alec Gross, Sr. I
met him with the others coming in the direction of the Court
House. A young man ran up and seized Alec Gross, saying,
"This is my father, and he shall not vote the Democratic
ticket." He was followed by at least a dozen other colored
men, who endeavored to take him from us. We brought him
along until we got into the gate leading to the Court House
yard at the Clerk's office, when he was by force taken from
us by the colored men, and carried in front of the Court
House, near the brick office. The man, Alec Gross, was
frightened, confused, and, I think, thoroughly intimidated.
I endeavored, at the Court House gate, to allay the excitement, which was then very great. I saw Mr. Enos Pumphrey,

who was at that time a Deputy Sheriff, and urged upon him the propriety of quelling the excitement. He went into the crowd, and after awhile it seemed to quiet down. After Mr. Pumphrey did what I requested him to do, I came into the Court House yard, where, near the door leading into the Court House, I saw Captain Widdicombe, one of the candidates for Clerk. I requested him to go out and stop the excitement, as I thought his presence would have great weight in dispelling the colored men, who outnumbered the white men in the crowd surrounding Alec Gross. He told me that he had been out there, and endeavored to quiet them, but failed; that he had seen Alec, who told him that he wanted to vote the Democratic ticket, and that he, Widdicombe, then left the crowd. I thanked him for so doing; told him that I was much obliged to him, and shook him by the hand. I saw Gross about ten minutes after, at Mr. Turner's corner; he was greatly agitated, and scarcely knew what to say or do. His son, Alec Gross, Jr., and other colored persons, had entire control of him. I did not see him afterwards that day.

Cross-examined:

1st *Question.*—Do you or not know whether Mr. William B. Bowie was not allowed, after you say the crowd had Alec Gross in possession, to take him to the polls, and if he, Gross, had so desired, if he could not have voted as he pleased?

I did not see Mr. Bowie with Gross at all that day, and I do not think that Gross could have voted at all from the time he came to Marlboro', up to the time I saw him last, which was about 1 o'clock.

2d *Question.*—Was not the excitement of which you spoke caused by the contest going on between both parties as to which should take the old man Gross to the polls to vote, and did not Mr. Pumphrey rescue him from the Republicans, and assure him that he should vote as he desired?

The contest originated by Alec Gross, Jr., saying that his father should not vote the Democratic ticket, which was followed up by a crowd of colored men attempting to take him by force from the Democrats, and they finally succeeded in taking him away from us; it was a contest as to which side should vote him, after the remark made by his son. I do not .

know whether or or not Mr. Pumphrey rescued him or offered him any assurance as to how he should vote.

3d Question.—Do you know whether or not the agitation of Alec Gross at Turner's corner was not caused by a change of mind which had taken place after his talk with his son, and because of a fear if he did not vote the Democratic ticket, as he had promised to do, he might lose his place?

The first intimation I had of his desire to vote the Democratic ticket was from the remark of his son, who repeatedly said that he should not vote it, as well as the other colored ones in the crowd. The agitation referred to by me was nothing more nor less than the effect of the interference and intimidation that had been used against him from the time that he got out of the wagon until I last saw him. I know nothing of any conversation between the father and the son in regard to the old man's losing his place if he did not vote the Democratic ticket. I know nothing about it.

4th Question.—Was there not ample opportunity and time between the opening and closing of the polls on the 4th of November, 1873, for any one wishing to vote to do so, if he chose to remain during the day, and wait until the crowd had voted?

I think there was ample time and opportunity for parties to vote, if they had thought proper to subject themselves to the indignities and reproaches that were offered on that day; I do not think that Alec Gross could have been persuaded to vote at all at the time that I saw him, for the reasons I have given above.

5th Question.—Was there not a period of several hours in the afternoon when there was no difficulty of access to the polls; any one desiring to vote could do so without interference?

I think there was a period of an hour or so when parties could vote if they saw proper to do so, under the influences I have stated above.

6th Question.—Do you know of any one who voted at said election in your district, or elsewhere in the county, who had not been registered, or of any qualified voters offering to vote on said day of election, whose vote was refused by the Judges?

I can not speak of the voting out of my district ; I do not know of any one in my own district?

C. C. MAGRUDER, JR.

Test: JAMES HARRIS.

Thereupon adjourned until half-past nine o'clock to-morrow morning.

————

JANUARY 7th, 1874.

Met pursuant to adjournment.

There being no witness in attendance, adjourned until 9½ o'clock to-morrow morning.

————

JANUARY 8th, 1874.

Met pursuant to adjournment.

DEPOSITION No. 32.

GEORGE W. WILSON, JR., being duly sworn, deposes as follows :

1st Question.—State your name, age, occupation, place of residence, and where you voted on the 4th day of November, 1873.

My name is George W. Wilson, Jr. ; age, 29 years ; occupation, merchant ; reside at Upper Marlboro', and voted in the Third Election District on the 4th day of November, 1873.

2d Question.—Do you or do you not know of any interference by parties, with any voter or voters on the day of said election, and do you or do you not know of any intimidation of voters at the same ; if yea, state all you know about it?

I remember the case of Alec ; his other name I don't remember ; he resides, I think, at Wm. P. Pumphrey's ; he came here with his ticket, and got as far as the office, in front of the Court House, and he was surrounded by a crowd of black men, and there was considerable disturbance ; he was pushed and jostled about, and said that he was afraid to go any further ; that it was as much as his life was worth to go any further. I do not think he voted. There came very near being a riot, and I was called on by Mr. Pumphrey, the Constable, to help him to arrest a man ; I got the man on the ground, and was pulled off ; by whom, I don't know. I know of no intimidation. I know a negro who was bailed out of jail; I think his name is Tom ———, who told me that morning that he was afraid to vote; I do not know whether he voted or not.

Cross-examined :

1st Question.—Do you or not know of any one who was prevented, by violence or intimidation, from voting at the election held on the 4th day of November, 1873?

I do not positively, but believe that the man Alec was.

2d Question.—Was there not ample opportunity and time between the opening and closing of the polls on the 4th day of November, 1873, for any one wishing to vote to do so, if he chose to remain during the day, and wait until the crowd had voted?

If a man had not been afraid, there was ample time.

3d Question.—Do you know of any one who voted at said election, in your district or elsewhere in the county, who had not been registered?

I do not.

GEO. W. WILSON, JR.

Test : JAMES HARRIS.

———

JANUARY 9th, 1874.

Met pursuant to adjournment.

There being no witnesses in attendance, continued until 9½ o'clock, to-morrow morning.

———

JANUARY 10th, 1874.

Met pursuant to adjournment.

DEPOSITION No. 33.

STALEY N. MAGRUDER, first being duly sworn, deposes as follows :

1st Question.—State your name, age, occupation, place of residence, and where you voted on the 4th day of November, 1873?

My name is Staley N. Magruder; age, 60 years; occupation, farmer; reside in Prince George's County, Bladensburg District, and I voted in the Second Election District, on the 4th day of November, 1873.

2d Question.—Were you or not Registrar of voters in said district during the year 1873?

I was.

3d Question.—As such Registrar, did you or not register three white men as qualified voters on the last day of registration, and subsequently erase their names from the registration book without their knowledge or consent, and without their being apprised of the fact until the day of election? If yea, state the names of the parties so erased, and the reasons which induced you to do the same. State fully all you know on the subject.

I did. Charles H. Walker was one; Charles H. Dickenson and Patrick Ferquher. My reason for doing so was this: I will take Dickenson first; Mr. Dickenson was employed in the county as agent for some Sewing Machine Company: he was a Virginian by birth; he moved his family to the City of Washington and moved them thence in June last to the county, and he said that he had been a resident of the county for twelve months to last October. He made his case out pretty fair to his own idea, and then he left it to me to do it. I did hesitate sometime before I registered his name. He was not present when I registered his name; this was before the last days of registration, I think. After reflecting upon and before the books went out of my hands, I considered that he had no residence and struck his name from the books; it was after serious reflection that I did so. Mr. Charles Walker was the next; his statement was that his family did not live in the county, nor never had, but he owned property in the county, and had been employed in carrying on a mill for two years in the county, but had not voted for two years any where. I put his name down on the very last day and in his presence, and just before I closed the book, and, upon reflection, I struck his name off. Patrick Ferquher was an Irishman; he stated that he had been in the country twenty-four years and had voted, but had no naturalization or transfer papers, and, upon reflection, I struck his name off. I had registered his name in his presence. I struck all three of their names off out of their presence, because I thought the law was against me. Two of them had no residence, in my opinion, and the other had not the proper papers. These parties were not notified that their names

were stricken off, because I did not think the law requires it ;
although I thought it my duty, through an act of courtesy,
to do so.

Cross-examined :

1st Question.—Did you strike off the names referred to by
you above, because you thought they would vote the Democratic ticket, or would you not have done the same thing in
compliance with law, as you understood it, if they had been
Republicans ; and did you not act as your conscience dictates
and as the law requires ?

I did. My impression was that they would vote the
Democratic ticket, but I did not know positively how they
would vote. I am a Democrat myself.

2d Question.—As Registrar, did you give any notice to the
Judges of Election that you had improperly registered any
man and afterwards stricken off his name ; and if not, why did
you not give such notice ; and were not those names stricken
off before making out your list and before said books had been
returned to the Clerk of the Circuit Court ? Was not said election conducted fairly in your opinion ?

I did not give any such notice to the Judges of Election,
because the books were sealed until the day of election, and I
thought I would let things take their course. They were
stricken off before the books were returned to the clerk, and
before the list was sent to the Judges of Election. Said election was conducted as fair as usual, in my opinion. I came
away about one o'clock.

STALEY N. MAGRUDER.

Test: JAMES HARRIS.

Thereupon adjourned until twelve o'clock M., Monday,
January 12, 1874.

———

JANUARY 12th, 1874.

Met pursuant to adjournment.

No witnesses being in attendance, continued until to-morrow,
9½ o'clock A. M.

———

JANUARY 13th, 1874.

Met pursuant to adjournment.

No witnesses being in attendance, continued until to-morrow morning, 9½ o'clock.

JANUARY 14th, 1874.

Met pursuant to adjournment.

No witnesses being in attendance, adjourned until to-morrow, 9½ o'clock A. M.

JANUARY 15th, 1874.

Met pursuant to adjournment.

No witnesses being in attendance, continued until to-morrow morning, 9½ o'clock.

JANUARY 16th, 1874.

Met pursuant to adjournment.

No witnesses being in attendance, adjourned until to-morrow morning, 9½ o'clock.

JANUARY 17th, 1874.

Met pursuant to adjournment.

No witnesses being in attendance, continued until 9½ o'clock A. M., Monday, January 19th, 1874.

JANUARY 19th, 1874.

Met pursuant to adjournment.

No witnesses being in attendance, continued until to-morrow morning, 9½ o'clock.

JANUARY 20th, 1874.

Met pursuant to adjournment.

No witnesses being in attendance, continued until to-morrow morning, 9½ o'clock.

JANUARY 21st, 1874.

Met pursuant to adjournment.

No witnesses being in attendance, adjourned until 9½ o'clock A. M., to-morrow.

JANUARY 22d, 1874.

Met pursuant to adjournment.

No witnesses being in attendance, adjourned until to-morrow morning, 9½ o'clock.

JANUARY 23d, 1874.

Met pursuant to adjournment.

There being no witnesses in attendance, adjourned until 9½ o'clock to-morrow morning.

———

JANUARY 24th, 1874.

Met pursuant to adjournment, and adjourned until 12 o'clock M., Monday, January 26th, 1874.

———

JANUARY 26th, 1874.

Met pursuant to adjournment.

DEPOSITION No. 34.

A. T. BROOKE, having been first duly sworn, deposes as follows:

1st Question.—State your name, age, occupation, place of residence, and where you voted on the 4th of November, 1873?

My name is Augustus T. Brooke; age, 30, the 9th of March, 1874; clerk; residence, Upper Marlboro', and voted in the Third Election District, Prince George's County.

2d Question.—Did you or not see parties acting as clerks of election at said polls who were not duly qualified? If yea, give their names.

I did. I acted myself a portion of the day. I saw Thomas E. Williams and Charles C. West, both acting as such. I was not sworn in, and acted at the request of the Judges. I know that the others were not sworn in during the day. I saw the Judges swear Mr. Williams in after the polls were closed. No one said any thing to me about being sworn in, and I think not to Mr. West.

3d Question.—Did you or not have a conversation with George Bowling in regard to voting in this county? If yea, state the same and when it occurred.

I did. It was on the 6th of November, 1873; two days after the election. I met George Bowling in the Court House yard. He commenced the conversation by saying he regretted very much he had to vote against my brother at the election. I told him that I was rather surprised to see him here voting at all. He said that he heard that his name was still on the registration book, and he thought he might as well come down and vote, but that it was the last time that he ever expected to vote here. He said that he left here with the intention of returning to live here. I then asked him if he considered himself a resident of this place or the county ; to which he gave no direct answer—neither admitting or denying the same.

[The last question and the answer thereto was excepted to, for the reason that neither notice served upon Robert S. Widdicombe, or his attorney, contained any statement that such question would be asked or proof given.]

4th Question.—Do you or not know how long since the Rev. L. J. Evans, colored, removed from this county, and whether he voted here at the late election ?

I do. It was last winter ; either in January or February. I saw him vote here.

5th Question.—Do you or not know how long Charles Marshall has been out of the county, and where he lived at the time of the election ?

He has been out of the county for about eighteen or twenty months. He told me the night before the election that he was living in Washington.

6th Question.—Do you know how long H. Eugene Brooke and Albert Brooke have been residing in Washington City, and whether, since they removed there, they have only visited the county at long intervals and for short periods of time. Have you not been intimate with said parties, and prior to the late election did you ever hear either express the intention of returning to this county to reside?

I know that H. Eugene Brooke has been living in Washington for nearly four years ; that Albert Brooke has been living there for upwards of two years ; I have seen them in the county quite often during that time, on visits of both long and short duration ; I have been intimate with said parties, and never heard them express any intention of returning to Prince George's County to live.

7th Question.—Do you know in what election district of said county the farm, whereon the mother of these parties formerly resided, is situated, and how do you know it ?

I have always heard that it was in the Fourth Election District, and have seen upon the assessment books of this county that the farm is assessed in said Fourth Election District.

Cross-examined:

1st Question.—What relation are you to the Contestant in this case, and are you not his chief clerk?

I am his brother and his chief clerk.

2d Question.—Do you know whether you acted in violation of law in acting as Clerk to the Judges of the Election without being sworn?

I do not know.

3d Question.—Did you, whilst acting as such clerk, do anything, to your knowledge, in violation of law, and did you not faithfully perform your duty while acting as such clerk?

I did not do anything in violation of law, and performed my duty to the best of my ability.

4th Question.—How do you know that neither Mr. Williams nor Mr. West were not sworn in by the Judges of Election upon assuming the duties of clerk to the same?

I was present when they were called upon by the Judges, and did not see them administer any oath to them; I presume they did not previously, as they swore Mr. Williams in as clerk after the polls were closed; they had been acting during the day.

5th Question—Do you know whether the Rev. Lewis Evans removed permanently from the county or not?

I don't know; he is a Methodist preacher, and presume that he has no permanent residence anywhere.

6th Question.—Do you know whether Charles Marshall has been back to the county since he first removed? And, if so, how often?

I do; I have seen him here twice last summer, and at the time of election.

7th Question.—Do you know whether Eugene Brooke and Albert Brooke have been voting in Prince George's County for the last four years, or for how long a time?

I have seen them vote here for several years, except the election held in 1872, on which day I saw neither one of them here, and do not think that they voted.

8th Question.—Do you not know that Mr. Eugene Brooke

intended to vote here at the election in 1872, but was prevented by an accident?

I do not.

A. T. BROOKE.

Test : JAMES HARRIS.

DEPOSITION No. 35.

WILLIAM H. HARPER, having been first duly sworn, deposes as follows:

1st Question.—State your name, age, occupation, place of residence and where you voted at the election held on the 4th of November, 1873?

My name is William H. Harper; age, 33 years; druggist, and reside in Upper Marlboro', and where I voted on the 4th day of November, 1873.

2d Question.—Have you or not had any conversations with George Bowling, since he left here, in regard to returning to this county to live? If yea, please state the same.

I have; I had a conversation with him in Washington; he commenced the conversation and told me that he never intended to come back here to live, and advised me to leave Prince George's County also; this conversation occurred in the fall of 1872.

3d Question.—Do you know how long H. Eugene Brooke and Albert Brooke have been residing in Washington City, and whether, since they have removed there, they have only visited the county occasionally? Have you not been intimate with said parties, and, prior to the late election, did you ever hear either of them express the intention of returning here to reside?

Eugene went there either the latter part of 1869 or the first part of 1870; I can't say which. He was in business, first by himself, and afterwards took Mr. Drury in with him. Albert left when his mother left, and I think she left in 1870. The only home he had was with her; and since they left they have only visited the county occasionally. I have been intimate with said parties, and I never heard either of them, prior to the election, express any intention of returning to the county to reside.

7.

Cross-examined:

1st Question.—Do you know where H. Eugene Brooke has been voting for the last several years during his stay in Washington?

He has been voting in Prince George's County.

2d Question.—Do you or not know Wm. H. Queen, commonly called "Polk Queen," and whether or not he voted in the Third Election District of Prince George's County on the 4th of November, 1873, and whether he voted for Robert S. Widdicombe or Henry Brooke, the Contestant?

I do know Wm. H. Queen, and do not know whether he voted or not.

3d Question.—Did you hear him say whether he intended to vote for Mr. Brooke or Mr. Widdicombe, and do you know of any one giving him a ticket with Mr. Brooke's name upon it, and did he consent to vote the same?

He told me that he wanted to vote for Mr. Brooke; that he came down here more for that purpose than anything else. He went into my store, and I made out a ticket for him, it being an entire Republican ticket, except that Mr. Brooke's name was upon it, and he intended to vote the same.

Re-cross-examined:

1st Question.—Was not the ticket you gave Queen a Democratic ticket, with the names of the Republican candidates written upon it?

It was.

. Have you not examined the ballots of Marlboro' District, and failed to find that ticket among them, and did you not see said Queen vote?

I have not examined them myself; I understand that it was not among them. I heard that it was taken away from him in the yard. I did not see him vote.

W. H. HARPER.

Test: James Harris.

The Contestant now files with me the papers herewith returned, marked "Exhibits 1, 2, 3, 4, 5, 6, 7, 8, 9, 10, 11, 12, 13, 14 and 15," purporting to be certified extracts from the poll and registration books of Prince George's County, a copy of the returns of election of 1873 in said

county, a copy of the Docket Entries in the case of the State
vs. Worthington, and of the presentment in the same case, in
the Circuit Court for said county ; and also the Docket Entries
in the cases of the State vs. George Locker ; same vs. Nace
Beall, and same vs. Mack Johnson.

Mr. Robert S. Widdicombe afterwards filed with me the
paper herewith returned, marked " R. S. W., No. 1 ;" to
which the said Henry Brooke filed a response, also herewith
returned, marked " H. B."

Neither party desiring to make any further interrogatories,
or producing any other witnesses, I accordingly close this
testimony, and certify that the foregoing is a true statement
of answers given by the several witnesses as they were re-
spectively produced and examined before me.

Given under my hand and seal, this 26th day of January,
Anno Domini, 1874.

[L. S.] JAMES HARRIS,
Justice of the Peace.

STATE OF MARYLAND, PRINCE GEORGE'S COUNTY, SCT :

I HEREBY CERTIFY, That James Harris, Esq., before whom
the annexed depositions were taken, and who has thereto subscribed his name, was, at the time of so doing, a Justice of
the Peace of the State of Maryland, in and for the County of
Prince George's, duly commissioned and sworn.

In Testimony Whereof, I hereto set my hand and affix the
seal of the Circuit Court for Prince George's County, this
26th day of January, Anno Domini, 1874.

HENRY BROOKE,
Clerk of the Circuit Court for Prince George's County.

To THE PRESIDING OFFICER OF THE
          HOUSE OF DELEGATES OF THE STATE OF MARYLAND:
Sir :

In accordance with the provisions of the 61st Section of the 35th Article of the Maryland Code of Public General Laws, I herewith transmit a certificate of notices and proof of the service of the same, and the deposition taken in the Contested Election Case therein named.

Respectfully,   RUFUS BELT,
Justice of the Peace of the State of Maryland, in and for Prince George's County.

To HENRY BROOKE, ESQ. :

Sir—You are hereby notified that in accordance with Section 52, of Article 35, of the Code of Public General Laws of Maryland, as amended by the Act of 1865, chapter 143, relating to contested elections, Robert S. Widdicombe, whose election as Clerk of the Circuit Court for Prince George's County, under the election held on the 4th day of November, 1873, you are contesting, has applied to the undersigned, a Justice of the Peace of the State of Maryland, in and for the County of Prince George's aforesaid, for a notice under my hand and seal, to be directed to you, notifying you that he will examine before me the following persons as witnesses, who are hereinafter named, to wit :

H. Eugene Brooke, Albert Brooke, George Bowling, Sam'l Williams, Charles Marshall, Wm. H. Queen, Wm. Orme, John McNally, Wm. Allen, Francis Allen, Solomon Chany, Joseph H. Bell, R. H. Beall, Geo. Marshall, Edward Riley, Barney West, Wm. H. Harper, Jas. B. Belt, Jere. Ryon, Arthur Tolson, Samuel Brown, Matthew Johnson, Philip Jones, Robert Carroll, Fielder C. Duval, James H. Parker, Samuel Jennings, John Ridout, Benj. Fletcher, Sr., Benj. Fletcher, Jr., Eli S. Prime, Wm. Wallace, Geo. W. Jackson, Alex. Gross, Jr., Geo. F. Eberly, Thos. H. Jackson,

Daniel A. Jenkins, John Wood, Alex. Barns, Thos. Holland, Lewis Johnson, Theophilus Johnson, Richard H. Sansbury, B. Frank Duvall, John E. Gardner, Lemuel Porter, James Flint, John W. Duvall, Benedict Yost, George C. Merrick, Geo. Locker, Edward Jones, Benj. I. Gwynn, Frederick W. Foulke, Peter G. Grimes, Alex. Gross, Sr., Jas. T. Perkins, Alonzo Darcy, Mordecai Stamp, Chas. Stewart, John Thomas, Oden Williams, Geo. Tenley.

By whom he expects to prove—

First. That H. Eugene Brooke, Albert Brooke, Geo. Bowling, Charles Marshall, Joseph H. Beall, Geo. W. Jackson, Frederick W. Foulke, Samuel Williams, Wm. Orme, and Wm. H. Queen, John McNally, Francis Allen, and Minor Pose were not disqualified as voters in Prince George's County, on the 4th day of November, 1873, on the ground of non-residence.

Second. That Ambrose Carroll, Hamilton Carroll, and Henry Holland were 21 years of age on the 4th day of November, 1873, or prior thereto.

Third. That Mack Johnson, Nace Beall, and George Locker were not unpardoned convicts on the 4th day of November, 1873, and thereby disqualified from voting.

Fourth. That Aquilla Wilson, John W. Lowe, Daniel Clarke, George Hammond, Robert Oliver, John Buckmaster, Joseph Withers, Michael Sparrow, H. Brune Bowie, C. C. Hyatt, Jr., Carter Hall, W. W. W. Bowie, Oden Mulliken, John Francis Mudd, John D. Seitz, T. Thompson, Chas. G. Addison, Walter Addison, J. Lack Higgins, being non-residents of said county, were permitted to vote and did vote for Henry Brooke, the Contestant, at the election held in Prince George's County, on the 4th day of November, 1873.

Fifth. That Thomas A. Hyde, an unpardoned convict, did vote for the Contestant in the Third Election District of Prince George's County, on the 4th of November, 1873.

Sixth. That Ammond Shaffer voted in the Second Election District, in Prince George's County, on the 4th day of November, 1873, for Henry Brooke, the Contestant, the said Shaffer being, at the time of casting his vote, a minor.

Seventh. That, owing to intimidation and other unlawful interference, legally qualified voters were prevented from voting for Robert S. Widdicombe, for Clerk of the Circuit Court for Prince George's County, at the election held on the 4th day of November, 1873, to wit: Thos. H. Jackson, Barney West, Major Coats, Wm. Shorter, and Butler Snow.

Eighth. That James Oakey, Oden Williams, Chas. Stewart, Alex. Gross, Sr., and Washington Johnson were not prevented by intimidation or other illegal causes, from voting the Democratic ticket, or for Henry Brooke, the Contestant, at the election held on the 4th day of November, 1873.

And you are further notified that the said Robert S. Widdicombe shall offer in evidence certified copies and extracts from the poll and registration books of the respective districts of said county.

You are, therefore, hereby notified to attend, in person or by attorney, at the Court House, in the town of Upper Marlboro', on Monday, the 19th day of January, 1874, at 12 o'clock, M., to cross-examine witnesses, and do such other matters in the premises as you desire; and you are further notified if such testimony cannot be taken on the day named, the taking of the same will be continued from day to day until the same is completed.

Given under my hand and seal this 7th day of January, 1874.

.[L. S.]   RUFUS BELT,
                           Justice of the Peace.

1874, January 7th. Service admitted.

            C. C. MAGRUDER, JR.,
             Attorney for H. BROOKE, *Contestant.*

DEPOSITION No. 1.

ALBERT BROOKE being sworn, deposes as follows:

1st Question.—State your name, age, residence, and in what election district you voted on the 4th of November, 1873?

My name is Albert Brooke; thirty-four years of age next birth-day; resident of Prince George's, and voted in the Third Election District.

2d Question.—Please state how long you have voted in this county and district, and have you ever voted or offered to vote elsewhere?

I voted in Prince George's, Third Election District, since 1866, and I have never voted or offered to vote elsewhere.

3d Question.—Was your name on the list of registered voters and on the poll-book on the 4th of November, 1873, and did the Judges of Election receive and deposit your vote in the ballot-box on the said election day without objection?

My name was on the registration list and also the poll-book, and my vote was received without a murmur and deposited in the box.

4th Question.—How long have you resided in this county, and have you ever lost your residence in the county?

I have resided in the county since 1865; I never have lost my residence.

5th Question.—Did you, or did you not, tell Mr. Wm. B. Bowie that you had removed from this county about two years since or at any other time?

I never did.

6th Question.—Do you know or do you not know John Buck-master; if so, state if you saw him at the polls on the 4th day of November, 1873; state further if he voted and if you know how he voted?

I know John Buckmaster; I saw him at the polls; he came at my solicitation to vote for Mr. Brooke, and told me he had done so.

7th Question.—Please state if you have any objection to state how you voted and for whom you voted for clerk on the 4th of November, 1873?

I voted the Republican ticket with the exception of Henry Brooke, for whom I voted for Clerk of the Circuit Court.

8th Question.—Was there or was there not ample time between the opening and the closing of the polls on the 4th of November, 1873, for all persons desiring to vote to do so, without hindrance or obstruction; and was not the result of the election on that day a fair discussion of the sentiments of the legally qualified voters; and do you know of any person whose name does not appear upon the list of qualified voters, as returned by the officer of registration, who voted at said election?

From the time I arrived in Marlboro', which was about half-past ten or eleven o'clock, I observed no hindrance in any manner, and I think the time was ample; I think the expression was fair; I see no reason why it was not; I do not know of any person, whose name does not appear upon the list of qualified voters, who voted.

9th Question.—Are you acquainted with H. Eugene Brooke and George Bowling, and do you know where they reside?

I am acquainted with Eugene Brooke and George Bowling; they have always claimed Prince George's as their residence, and I am satisfied that they never voted or offered to vote any where else.

Cross-examined:

1st Question.—Please give your present post-office address; state how long it has been such, and what your address was previous thereto?

My post-office address is just where I am supposed to be; previous to the 7th day of this month one year ago it was Fairfield, St. Mary's Co., Md.; at present, while I am in Washington, my letters are directed there.

2d Question.—Please state how long you were removed from the county, and what length of time you have passed in Prince George's County for the last three years?

I do not consider I ever moved from Prince George's; I have been in Prince George's at different periods, and elsewhere as I could obtain employment, but never remained at any point long enough to acquire a vote elsewhere; I suppose I have been in the county for the last three years, one year or over at different times.

3d Question.—When were you last employed in Prince George's?

I consider that I am employed in Prince George's at present.

4th Question.—In what capacity and when were you so employed?

I was employed about May, 1872, since which time I have been in the employ of the Washington City and Point Lookout Railroad Company, which work is now being constructed.

5th Question.—Has your employment in said capacity been continuous since May, 1872, and what period of time has that employment required your presence in Prince George's County?

It has been continuous. I have passed no time in Prince George's County in the employment of said Company.

6th Question.—State where you passed said time in said employment?

Portion of the time in St. Mary's County, portion in Washington City and a portion en route between the two points.

7th Question.—State where you reside in Prince George's County; whether you are housekeeping, or with whom yourself and family live, and how long have you lived there?

I claim my residence in the Third Election District, and have never claimed it anywhere else; and have as much residence there as I have at any other point upon the top of God's green earth. I am not housekeeping or boarding any where; myself and family are not living at any particular point at this particular time. I have been sojourning for a time with my mother—within the last two years—I suppose I have been there about eight months at different times.

8th Question.—Did you see many strangers at the polls in Third Election District on the said day of election, and do you know from whence they came?

I saw several persons on the day of election whom I did not know. I have no idea from whence they came or where they were bound.

9th Question.—Please state when H. Eugene Brooke commenced business in Washington, whether he sold out his farm here prior to that time, and whether he took his wife to Washington with him then?

I don't exactly know what time he commenced business in Washington; I suppose about three years ago; he did sell his farm prior to the time he carried his wife with him, where she has been with him ever since.

10th Question.—Please state if you know when George Bowling closed his business here and took his family to Washington, and if you know if he has ever been in the county since, except upon a visit?

I don't know when he closed his business here; I know that his family is there at present, but do not know how long they have been there. I have seen him in the county frequently since. I am not prepared to say how long he remained at any particular time.

Re-examination :

1st Question.—State, if you please, whether H. Eugene Brooke and yourself have not voted at nearly every election held in Prince George's County since 1866, and whether any objection was ever raised to your voting in said county so long as he and yourself were identified with the Democratic party?

Both H. Eugene Brooke and myself have voted in Prince George's since 1866, and no objection has ever been made. I never was identified with the Democratic party. I never heard of any objection to H. Eugene Brooke voting.

ALBERT BROOKE.

Test: RUFUS BELT.

DEPOSITION No. 2.

1st Question.—State your name, residence, age and at what election district you voted on the 4th of November, 1873?

Name, George Bowling ; residence, Washington ; age, 56 ; voted in the Third Election District, Prince George's County.

2d Question.—How long have you voted in this county and district, and have you ever voted or offered to vote elsewhere?

I have voted in this county and district since 1870 ; I have never voted or offered to vote elsewhere.

3d Question.—Was your name on the list of registered voters and on the poll-book on the 4th day of November, 1873, and did the Judges of the Election receive and deposit your vote in the box, on the said election day, without objection?

I was on the books ; they did receive and deposit my ballot without objection.

4th Question.—How long have you resided in this county, and have you ever lost your residence here?

I have lived in this county since the Spring of 1841 ; I have not lost my residence here.

5th Question.—Were you not, on the 4th day of November, 1873, and are you not now, a property-holder in Prince George's County, and only temporarily staying in Washington City until you could have a dwelling built upon said property in Prince George's County?

I am and was, on the day of election, a property-holder ; I partly bargained with Mr. Clark to build me a house at Seabrooke ; I was only living in Washington temporarily.

6th Question.—Did you or did you not tell Mr. Wm. B. Bowie, about two years ago, or at any other time, that you had removed from Prince George's County?

Yes, sir; I told him I had moved from the county because I had nothing to do here; but I told him I considered it my residence.

7th Question.—Do you or not know Charles Marshall, Wm. Orme, Samuel Williams, Wm. H. Queen? And, if so, state where they claim their residence, and if you know them to have been qualified voters on the 4th day of November, 1873?

I do know all of them; they claim Prince George's County for their residence.; I believe them to have been qualified voters on the 4th of November, 1873.

8th Question.—Do you or not know Minor Pose? If so, state where you suppose his residence to have been on the said day of election, and state what he said to you about his residence and voting?

I do know Minor Pose; he was working anywhere he could get work to do; he never intended to leave Prince George's; he always intended to come here and vote.

Cross-examination:

1st Question.—State when you took your family to Washington, broke up house-keeping here, and if you have been temporarily staying with your family in Washington since?

This September gone, two years, I took my family to Washington to reside temporarily; I have been living with my family ever since, temporarily, but I bought property here before I left, so as not to lose my residence; intended to return and remain as soon as my house was built.

2d Question.—Do you know how long Charles Marshall, William Orme, Samuel Williams and Wm. H. Queen have been temporarily employed in Washington? If yea, please state when each of them went there?

Chas. Marshall has been in Washington about twelve months, I think, to the best of my knowledge; Mr. Orme I met there last September; don't know how long he had been there; Samuel Williams I saw there last March for the first time, but he came back to the county again; Wm. H. Queen I saw in Washington last August.

3d Question.—Do you know where Minor Pose resided, and

with whom, before he went to Washington, and if ever he resided in Spalding's District?

He said he lived with Mr. Robert Clagett, in Marlboro'
District; don't know that he ever lived in Spalding's.

4th Question.—Do you know, of your own knowledge, if
either of these parties ever registered or voted, or offered to
register or vote, in any other place excepting Prince George's
County?

I do not know.

5th Question.—State, if you know, at what numbers and on
what streets in Washington each of these parties were living
in September last?

I don't know.

6th Question.—Did you ever say in a conversation with any
one that you did not think your name was still on the registration books, but, learning that it was, you were induced to
come here and vote?

I do not remember; I was perfectly satisfied that it was;
did not think it necessary to answer any questions.

GEORGE BOWLING.

Test: Rufus Belt.

Deposition No. 3.

1st Question.—State your name, age, residence, and occupation, and in what election district you voted on the 4th of
November, 1873.

Joseph M. Beall; age, 50 years old the 5th of January; I
now temporarily reside in Washington; carpenter; I voted
in Bladensburg on the 4th of November, 1873.

[Objection filed to the above witness by Contestant, on the
ground that his name does not appear on the list of witnesses
furnished by R. S. Widdicombe. Ruled by the Justice that
it being a misnomer, he should testify.]

2d Question.—How long have you voted in this county, or
Bladensburg District, and have you ever voted or offered to
vote elsewhere?

I have voted in Bladensburg District since 1870,; I never
have voted or offered to vote elsewhere.

3d Question.—Was your name on the list of registered
voters and on the poll-book on the 4th of November, 1873,

and did the Judges of Election deposit your vote in the ballot-box on said day of election without objection?

My name was on the list of registered voters and the poll-book, and the Judges did receive my vote without objection.

4th Question.—Do you or not own property in Prince George's County, and if about two-thirds of your time is not spent in this county? Did you always consider that you had no right to register or vote anywhere else?

I do own property in this county; fully two-thirds of my time is spent in this county; I did not consider that I could register or vote elsewhere.

Cross-examination:

1st Question.—Are you not sojourning with your family in the District of Columbia, and if so, how long have you and they been there; and what is the number of your house, and the street upon which it is situated, or, if outside of the city limits, whereabouts is said dwelling?

When I am there I am with my family, but am seldom there; they have been there temporarily two years on the 4th of January last; house is on Fifth street, No. 1,318.

2d Question.—Have your family been residing at that house ever since they have been in the District of Columbia? And if not, give the number and street upon which they previously resided.

When I first went there they lived on the corner of F street and Tennessee avenue. I moved from there on the 14th of June, 1873; no number to the house.

3d Question.—Have you ever applied to be registered as a qualified voter in the District of Columbia?

I never applied to be registered.

4th Question.—How long have you owned property in this county, and do you not also own property in the District, where your family temporarily reside, or any other property?

I have owned property in this county since 1871. I expect to own the property where I reside, but I do not own any now in the District.

5th Question.—Did no one object to your voting in Bladens-burg at the last election, and did you ever remark that you did not think you could vote there, but were informed that your name had not been stricken off the registration book?

There was no objection to my voting ; have no recollection
of ever making such a remark.

JOSEPH M. BELL.

Test : RUFUS BELT.

DEPOSITION No. 4.

1st Question.—State your name, age, occupation, residence,
and where you voted on the 4th day of November, 1873.

Richard H. Sansbury ; age, 40 ; farmer and route agent ;
voted in the Third Election District ; residence, Third District,
Prince George's County.

2d Question.—Do you know of any non-residents who voted
the Democratic ticket or tickets in Prince George's County at
the election held on the 4th day of November, 1873, and if
so, give their name or names, and state all you know ?

Nothing more than temporary non-residents ; George Ham-·
mond, Lack Higgins, Robert Oliver and Joseph Withers.

3d Question.—How long have the parties to whom you refer
resided out of the county and State?

I do not know if they ever lived out of the State. At present
Higgins lives in Anne Arundel County ; he lived in Anne
Arundel County at the last election. The other parties never,
to my knowledge, resided in Prince George's County, but I
have never doubted their right to vote here.

4th Question.—Where does Mr. Oliver's family reside? Did
you ever know him to reside in Prince George's County ?

I never knew him to reside in Prince George's County.

5th Question.—Do you know where George Hammond resides, and did you ever know him to reside in Prince George's
County ?

I learn that his family reside in Anne Arundel County ;
I have never known him to reside in Prince George's County.

6th Question.—Do you or do you not know if these parties
voted, and, to the best of your knowledge and belief, state
how they voted ?

I believe they voted, and voted for Henry Brooke ; as for
the balance of the Democratic ticket, I do not know if they
voted it all, or not.

7th Question.—Do you know of any interference with Republican voters by Democrats, at the election held on the 4th

day of November, 1873, and do you know of any voter or voters who were prevented from voting the Republican ticket, by such intimidation or interference, on said day of election ; if so, give name or names, and state all you know about it?

I know of none.

8th Question.—Was there or not ample time for any person or persons desiring to vote to do so, and if any, who were those prevented from voting through fear, threats, or intimidation?

There was ample time for every one wishing to vote to do so. I know of no one being intimidated by threat.

9th Question.—Do you know of any person or persons who voted on said election day, whose name or names were not on the registration list of qualified voters ?

I know of none.

10th Question.—Was not the election, in your estimation, fairly conducted on the said day, 4th of November, 1873, and the public sentiment fairly expressed on that day, at the ballot-box ?

I believe the election was fairly conducted, and every man voted as he desired.

Cross-examination:

1st Question.—Do you know when George Hammond, Lack Higgins, Robert Oliver, and Joseph Withers came to this county, and have they not been in the employ of the Baltimore and Philadelphia Railroad Company here, ever since that time, or what period ?

I do not know when they came to this county ; when I first knew them they were in the employ of the Baltimore and Philadelphia Railroad ; I cannot state how long I have known them.

2d Question.—Do you think it has been one year, or less, since these parties first came to this county ?

I know it has been over a year since Oliver and Withers came here in the employ of the railroad company ; I think it has been less than a year since the others came in the county.

3d Question.—Do you know where either of these parties spend the most of their time ?

I do not know where they spend the most of their time, unless it be on the railroad, between Bowie and Pope's Creek.

4th Question.—Do you know if Hammond and Oliver are married, and to whom do you refer as their family?

I do not think they are married. I refer to their parents as their family.

5th Question.—Have you any personal knowledge as to where the family of either of these parties reside, and do you know how often either of said parties visits his family; whether frequently or not?

I only know what I have been told; do not know how often they visit their families; whether frequently or not.

6th Question.—Do you not run on the same train with some of these parties, and if so, which, and do you not see them nearly every day?

I run on the train with Higgins, but not with Oliver and Hammond; I see them every day nearly.

7th Question.—Did you see either of these parties vote at said election, and did you distinctly see the ticket that each of them voted, and are you positive that the name of Henry Brooke was upon all of them?

I saw Mr. Oliver and Mr. Hammond when they came here, but did not see them vote; did not see any of the others vote. I am not positive that the name of Henry Brooke was upon all of them; did not see the ticket of either of them, but from their conversation, am certain they voted for Brooke.

8th Question.—You say that Mr. Higgins was living in Anne Arundel County on the day of said election; do you know if he was there on said day, and if he is not rarely there for more than a very short period?

He told me he voted in Marlboro' District; don't know if he was in Anne Arundel County that day; he is only there a very short time; goes some Saturday nights and returns Monday mornings.

9th Question.—Did you ever know either of said parties, and which of them, to reside out of Prince George's; if so, where did they then reside, and for what period of time?

Only what persons told me; I have been told that Oliver resides in Charles County, for what period of time I don't know, but understood he was raised there; I have been told that Higgins never resided in Prince George's County; I don't think George Hammond's family ever resided in Prince

George's; I am told that Withers' family reside in Baltimore; I have heard that his family lived here previously; they may have been temporarily residing here; I can't say.

10th Question.—Do you know if either of said parties, and which of them, boards in this county?

Oliver and Hammond eat two meals each day in Charles County, and one in Prince George's; Higgins boards in this county?

11th Question.—Did you or not see a number of strangers at the polls in said Third Election District, on the day of election, endeavoring to influence voters for the Republican party, and if so, state if you know where said parties were from, and who they were?

There were some parties from Washington, whom I had seen before, on election day conversing with the colored people, for what object I can't really say; I do not recollect the names of the said parties.

12th Question.—Do you know if either of said parties was in the employ of the United States Government, and in what capacity?

I do not know.

13th Question.—Did you hear the address by a colored orator near the polls on said day of election; do you know who he was, and what was the object or purpose of his argument?

I did see a colored man from Washington making an address to a crowd in the Court House yard; I have forgotten his name; I did not tarry or stay, but to the best of my knowledge from what I heard, he was speaking of the rights of the colored people under the Constitution; I did not stay long to hear his speech.

14th Question.—How far from the Court House door was this colored man making his speech?

About twenty-five or thirty feet, south-west corner of the yard.

Re-examined:

1st Question.—In what election district do these parties whom you refer to in your answer reside, and have they, to your knowledge, any residence at all in any district in this county, and do not Hammond and Oliver spend their nights in Charles?

8

They reside in no particular district in Prince George's County; they spend their nights at Cox's Station, Charles County.

2d Question.—You stated that you saw several parties from Washington City in Marlboro' on the day of election, and that a certain colored orator was addressing the colored voters in explanation of their rights under the Constitution; were these parties, or any of them, using any threats or were they guilty of any conduct calculated to produce fear or intimidation, or rather were they not speaking in an advisory way or by way of advice?

I did see a colored orator from Washington, but his language was of a conciliatory tone, and was of advice; there was no language used by way of threats or intimidation; all to the contrary.

Re-cross-examined:

1st Question.—About what number of strangers on said election day did you see at the polls? Was not the advice you heard given by these and the colored orator, that parties should vote the Republican ticket?

I think there was about three, besides the band of music; the advice was to vote your sentiments; I heard them say, if you wish to vote for a Democrat, to go and vote; heard these remarks frequently.

Re-examination-in-chief:

1st Question.—You stated you saw three; do you not know that this band was detained on account of the cars leaving them?

I believe they were detained; they were left over from the mass-meeting the night before.

R. H. SANSBURY.

DEPOSITION No. 5.

1st Question.—State your name, age, occupation, place of residence and where you voted on the 4th day of November, 1873.

George Marshall, name; age, 28; residence, Marlboro' District; voted in Marlboro' District; occupation, laborer.

2d Question.—Do you or do you not know David White and Peter Greenleaf, and how long since they left the county, and did they leave it permanently or merely to get work? Tell all you know about them.

Peter Greenleaf is now in this district; I think he has been here ever since the election ; I think he and White both left here some time after the 4th of March ; they were both working here on the railroad, near Marlboro'. Peter Greenleaf lived with Mr. Cross before he went on the railroad. David White worked with Richard Chew.

3d Question.—They have never been out of the county to your knowledge, to acquire a residence elsewhere, and you saw them in and around Marlboro' frequently before the election?

They have never been out of the county to my knowledge to seek a residence, and I saw them frequently around and about Marlboro' before the election ; and they always claimed their residence here, so far as I know of; never voted any where else. He saw David White in Washington on the day of election. I am satisfied he did not vote there. I also saw Greenleaf there that night; do not think he voted. They were working there temporarily.

4th Question.—Do you or do you not know one Joseph Gallaway, and did he not tell you that he wanted to vote the Republican ticket, and if he had been let alone by Democrats, he would have voted it without difficulty ; and in voting the Republican ticket, he voted his true sentiments?

I do know Joseph Gallaway ; I heard him say that he did not intend to vote otherwise than the Republican ticket. He said that Dr. Sasscer called upon him about his promises, and he said he never promised to vote the Democratic ticket. I saw Dr. Sasscer take hold of him on the day of election and ask him if he did not promise to vote for Mr. Wilson. Mr. Wilson was close by at the time—it was Judge Wilson. The Doctor did not make any threats towards the old man, but told him he would know where to get his living hereafter, so not to depend on him ; he had him by the collar, but Mr. Wilson told him to let him alone. He was on his way to the polls to vote the Republican ticket, and would have voted it if he had not been interrupted by Dr. Sasscer ; and would have voted freely but for this interruption ; if he voted the Republican ticket, he voted his true sentiments.

Cross-examination :

1st Question.—Were you not at work in Washington City a considerable portion of last year, and only occasionally visited Marlboro' ?

I was in Washington a considerable portion of last year. I visited Marlboro' occasionally.

2d Question.—Do you or not know if the interruption of Joseph Gallaway, by Dr. Sasscer, prevented him from voting, and did he not remain in the ranks of the colored voters, or did he leave the same and accompany Dr. Sasscer ?

I told you before that I did not mean to say that he voted or did not vote. I don't know that the interruption of Dr. Sasscer prevented his voting ; he did not leave the ranks whilst I was there.

3d Question.—Do you know or not know where the said Joseph Gallaway resided on the day of election, and where he now resides ?

I think he was living on Dr. Sasscer's place the day of election. I think he is still there.

4th Question.—Do you know the number of the house and name of street where David White and Peter Greenleaf lived in Washington last year, or where either of them resided when in Washington last year ?

I do not know.

5th Question.—Do you know positively that neither of these parties ever applied for registration, or to vote, or voted elsewhere than in Prince George's County ?

I do not know.

6th Question.—When did Joseph Gallaway tell you that he had never promised Dr. Sasscer to vote for Mr. Wilson ?

I heard him say so the same day of election, in the evening.

7th Question.—How do you know that if Joseph Gallaway voted the Republican ticket he voted his true sentiments ?

I don't know that he voted the Republican ticket, but heard him say that he intended to do so, and judge from that that he would have voted his true sentiments.

8th Question.—Did you or not see any strangers at the polls in Marlboro' District, on the said day of election ? If yea, state how many, who they were, and whether or not they were talking to the colored voters and urging them to vote the Republican ticket?

I saw strangers at the polls on the day of election; there were two or three, or several—one they called Green and one Becket—I don't know that there were any more; I think they were from Washington; I did not see them urging the colored voters to vote the Republican ticket particularly.

9th Question.—Was there not a band of music, composed of colored men, at the Court House or thereabouts all day? How many composed said band, and was not a colored orator addressing the crowd, in advocacy of the Republican principles, in front of the Court House, whilst said election was going on?

There was a band of music around the Court House during the day; they were at Flint's Hotel the most of the time; I don't know how many composed the band; I did not see a colored orator addressing the crowd.

10th Question.—How long were you at work in Washington during last year?

I went to Washington the last day of May.

Re-cross-examination:

1st Question.—Did these parties, David White and Peter Greenleaf, either board or occupy houses temporarily while absent from the county, and never resided in Washington permanently?

I don't know; I suppose they always claimed this as their residence.

2d Question.—Has or has not yourself and family a permanent residence in Marlboro', and you merely went away to Washington on account of scarcity of work here after the failure of the tobacco season, and you are now at work here?

Yes, sir.

3d Question.—Did not the band of music that you speak of being here on election day come down the night previous to attend a meeting, and were left over, on account of their failure to make the morning train, and afterwards left Marlboro' in an ambulance before the close of the election?

Yes, sir.

GEORGE ^{HIS} ⋈ MARSHALL.
MARK.

Test: RUFUS BELT.

DEPOSITION No. 6.

1st Question.—State your name, age, residence, occupation, and where you voted on the 4th of November, 1873.

Name, Samuel R. Jennings.

[Samuel R. Jennings produced, and objected to as not upon the list as furnished by Robert S. Widdicombe. Ruled by the Justice a misnomer, and he was entitled to testify.]

My name is Samuel R. Jennings, but it appears on the registration list as Samuel Jennings ; I mostly sign my name as Samuel Jennings, and I am the man referred to ; age, 30 years on the 14th of April next ; residence at Mr. James Mullikin's, Prince George's County, Queen Anne's District ; occupation, a carpenter ; voted in Queen Anne's District on the 4th day of November, 1873.

2d Question.—Do you or do you not know Oden Williams and Charles Stewart, and where did they vote on the 4th day of November, 1873, and were they in any way intimidated from voting their sentiments, and tell all you know about it?

I do know Oden Williams and Charles Stewart ; they voted in the Seventh Election District, Queen Anne's ; they were not in any way intimidated ; I saw Charles Stewart a few days previous to the election ; he told me that they had reported it that he wanted to vote the Democratic ticket, but it had always been and was then his desire to vote the full Republican ticket, and if he voted at all he intended to vote that ticket ; I saw him again on the day of election at the polls, and he said that he had been collared by some of the Democratic men to vote the Democratic ticket, and some one said, give him a Democratic ticket, which he showed to me ; and I asked him if he wanted to vote that ticket ; he said no, he would go home without voting first ; then he showed me the Republican ticket, and asked me if that was the ticket I was going to vote ; I told him yes, and he asked me to see him' vote ; I saw him vote the same ticket which he showed me, and it was a Republican ticket, without changing it from either hand to the other, or putting either one in his pocket. I saw Oden Williams before the election and he told me, in a very joyful manner, that he was going down to help the Republican party ; I was in conversation with him this morning, and he told me he did do it by voting an open Republican ticket, holding it up by its corners, and saying to others that were at the window, as he approached, "take care this eagle fly in there."

3d Question.—Do you or do you not know one Butler Snow, and where did he vote on the 4th of November, 1873, and was he not intimidated from voting for Robert S. Widdicombe, for Clerk of the Circuit Court on the Republican ticket, by being turned from his home ; and if so, tell what you know?

I know Butler Snow ; he voted in the Seventh Election District. I was home in bed when I heard some one knock at the door, on the 4th day of November, 1873, and I asked who it was, and he said, "It is me ;" and my wife said, "It is grandfather ; get up and open the door." I got up and opened the door, and asked him to come in. He said he did not care to come in ; that he wanted to hurry back home ; he merely came to let me know that he couldn't go to Queen Anne to vote. I then asked him why ; he said because he couldn't. I then told him to come in, and I would make up a fire, and we would sit down and talk. He told me his reason was for not going to vote that Governor Bowie told him if he went to Queen Anne, and did not vote for Mr. Brooke and Mr. Clark, he should not come on his place again ; and if he did, when he returned from the election, bring a team and move his family. I told him then that he should go to Queen Anne, and vote for whom he wanted to ; he then said he wanted to vote a full Republican ticket, but he could not do it without being turned out of doors, and he said, "Better let it alone, and not vote for any one." He went down to the polls with the intention of voting the Republican ticket, as he stated to me, and they had him so confused in trying to get him to vote for those men, that he said he would not vote at all, but go back home ; with that I left him. I won't be certain whether he said he voted for both of the gentlemen or not, but he told me that he had to vote the way Mr. Bowie wanted him, or else lose his home.

Cross-examination :

1st Question.—Did Butler Snow tell you that Gov. Bowie threatened to turn him off his place if he voted the Republican ticket?

He told me that Governor Bowie told him if he did not vote for those two men he would.

2d Question.—Did he tell you when Governor Bowie made this threat, or where, or in the presence of whom?

He did not say in the presence of any one, but on his place, and the day before the election.

3d Question.—Who were the parties you allude to as having Butler Snow so confused on the day of election? Give the names of all you remember—what they said and how they acted.

I saw him in the presence of John P. Hopkins and Daniel Clark. When we came in Queen Anne we met with Mr. Hopkins; I stated the case to him, as Butler Snow stated it to me; his answer was, "Sam, may be Butler Snow wants to vote for these men, and you don't want him to do it." I said, "I want him to vote for whom he wants to vote." He said, "I know he wants to vote for Mr. Clark, and if he wants to vote for Clark and Mr. Brooke both, let him do it." I said, "Mr. Hopkins, he said he had split his ticket once, and received no benefit from it; that he never intended to do it again." And I said, "Don't over-persuade the man, or make him do anything against his desire, for you know it is wrong." He said, "I know he wants to vote for Mr. Clark and Brooke;" he said to me, "Let him go and do it, and you fix his ticket for him." And I said, "I will not change his ticket, except at his request." I left them then standing talking. The next one I saw him with was Mr. Clark, but I was not near enough to hear what they said. The old man said he wanted to vote the full Republican ticket; he told Mr. Hopkins in my presence. Mr. Hopkins would not submit to the old man voting his opinion, but repeatedly said, when he told him he wanted to vote the Republican ticket and none other, that he knew he wanted to vote for Messrs. Clark and Brooke; that they were his best friends; so was Mr. Bowie; and the man told him that he wanted to vote the same as I did; he said it did not make any difference if he did or not; that he could vote for these two men and be as much thought of; and, in my judgment, he did not intend to give the old man up until he consented to vote that way.

4th Question.—Did Mr. Hopkins have hold of Butler Snow,

or use any threats or intimidation to prevent his leaving him, and could not Butler Snow have gone to the polls with you and voted the Republican ticket, if he chose to do so?

When I left him and Mr. Hopkins he started to go with me; Mr. Hopkins caught hold of him and told him he wanted to have some talk with him, and I left him and Mr. Hopkins standing in the road together. I did not hear of any threats while in their presence.

5th Question.—Did Butler Snow appear to remain with Mr. Hopkins willingly or unwillingly, and was Mr. Hopkins' conduct rough or kind in requesting him to remain, that they might have some talk?

He did not appear to remain willingly, for he started to leave Mr. Hopkins with me, and he caught hold of him and told him to stay with him awhile; he wished to have some talk with him. Mr. Hopkins' conduct was not very kind, nor very rough; he swore at him, and told him he had time enough; told me to go on; he would send him around after awhile.

6th Question.—State, if you please, Mr. Hopkins' exact language?

Mr. Hopkins said, by G——, that he knew Butler Snow wanted to vote for these gentlemen, and he'd be d——d if it wasn't through me that he would not do it, and he knew that he could get him to submit to what he would say to him.

7th Question.—Was not the swearing rather directed to you than the said Snow?

In my opinion it was not.

8th Question.—Do you know with whom Butler Snow came to the polls, and was he not with Mr. Hopkins when you joined them?

He came from Mitchelsville in the wagon furnished by Benjamin Fletcher, Jr., myself, Benjamin Fletcher, and a crowd of others that met there for breakfast, and, after leaving the wagon in Queen Anne, we met Mr. Hopkins about seventy-five or one hundred yards from store, the first we saw of him that day.

9th Question.—Did you see Butler Snow vote that day, and by whom was he accompanied when he went up to deposit his ticket?

I do not remember of seeing him vote, or having any conversation with him until after he had voted.

10th Question.—Did you see Gov. Bowie with him during the day?

I did not see him.

11th Question.—Did you see either Oden Williams or Chas. Stewart vote that day?

I did see Charles Stewart vote; I did not see Oden Williams vote.

12th Question.—Did you see any Democratic tickets, or Republican tickets with the names of any Democratic candidates, taken away from the colored men on said election day, torn up or retained, and full Republican tickets given them in their stead?

The only case I saw of that kind was with Charles Stewart, who had a Democratic ticket and a Republican ticket, for I examined both, and handed them back to them again, and, of his own accord, he tore up the Democratic ticket and voted the Republican ticket.

Re-cross-examined:

1st Question.—Was not the Mr. Hopkins you refer to in your testimony a Democrat, and was not his manner toward you rough, and the language he used toward Butler Snow calculated to confuse and coerce him into voting against his sentiments?

He was a Democrat; his language was rough and calculated to coerce and confuse Butler Snow to vote against his wishes.

2d Question.—Were any Democratic tickets taken away from voters on the day of election, against their wishes?

I do not know of any; all that were taken were given up willingly.

SAMUEL R. JENNINGS.

Test: RUFUS BELT.

DEPOSITION No. 7.

1st Question.—State your name, age, residence, occupation, and where you voted on the 4th day of November, 1873.

Frederick F. Foulke; age, 22; residence, Prince George's County; surveyor, assisting the Engineer Corps; I voted in the Second Election District on the 4th day of November, 1873.

2d Question.—How long have you resided in this county, and have you voted any place else in the last three years?

I have resided in Prince George's County for the past three years, and have never voted anywhere else. ·

Cross-examination:

1st Question.—What period of time have you actually been in this county during the year prior to said election?

About ten months.

Re-cross-examined:

1st Question.—During the last three years you have not been out of the county to reside permanently, and during that time have always had a residence in the county?

I have, sir; to the question.

FREDERICK FOULKE.

Test: RUFUS BELT.

DEPOSITION No. 8.

1st Question.—State your name, age, residence, occupation, and where you voted on the 4th day of November, 1873.

My name is George W. Jackson; age, 29 years; occupation, Surveyor of Prince George's County; residence, Prince George's County; voted in the Second Election District on the 4th of November, 1873.

2d Question.—How long have you voted in this county or district, and have you ever offered to vote elsewhere?

I have voted in this county for about eight years; I have never offered to vote or voted elsewhere.

Cross-examination:

1st Question.—When did you sell out your farm in this county and remove to Washington, and have not your family been living there for the past year?

I sold my farm in November, 1871; moved to Washington; since that time my family have been spending their summer in the county; I, myself, have been nearly all the time in Prince George's County.

2d Question.—Have you been boarding or house-keeping in Washington during the time and at the time of the election, and for how long prior thereto?

I have been house-keeping in Washington since November, 1871. ·

3d Question.—Were you engaged in any business in Washington or in the county; and, if so, state what business and how long you have been engaged?

I have been engaged in no business in Washington since November, 1871; have been engaged in engineering and surveying, in Prince George's, Montgomery, St. Mary's and Charles Counties ever since.

Re-cross-examined:

1st Question.—After you sold your place in November, 1871, you removed your family to Washington simply for convenience, and with no intention of acquiring a residence there, considering Prince George's your voting residence; and you have never voted or offered to vote any where except in Prince George's County?

I answer affirmatively to the whole question.

2d Question.—Had you or had you not been engaged in Prince George's County continuously, for one year or more, prior to the day of election?

I have.

GEORGE W. JACKSON.

DEPOSITION No. 9.

1st Question.—State your name, age, residence, occupation, and where you voted on the 4th day of November, 1873.

My name is Alexander Gross, Sr.; I am over 50 years of age; my residence is in Marlboro' District; occupation, laborer; I did not vote at all?

2d Question.—Did you or did you not come to Marlboro' on the 4th day of November, 1873, for the purpose of voting a Republican ticket, and would you not have voted said ticket but for the interference of Democrats; and was not that the reason you did not vote, because you found that they, the Democrats, would not allow you to vote as you desired?

I did not intend to come at first, but when I did come, I made up my mind to vote the ticket I had always voted, which was the Republican ticket. Indeed, I would have voted the Republican ticket if the Democrats had not interfered with me; that was the reason I did not vote, because they would not let me vote as I desired.

3d Question.—Was it not always your desire and intention to vote a Republican ticket?

It always was my intention to vote the Republican ticket, and I hope to vote it until the day of my death.

4th Question.—Were you not pulled and hauled, and, in fact, injured by members of the Democratic party, in their efforts to secure your vote for the candidates of that party?

Yes; to the question.

Cross-examination:

1st Question.—With whom did you come to Marlboro' on that day?

I came here with Mr. Pumphrey, in his wagon.

2d Question.—Did you tell either of the Mr. Pumphreys that you wanted to vote the same ticket they voted?

I did not tell Mr. Pumphrey that, but told them I wanted to vote the ticket I had always voted, but I did not want to come in to the polls.

3d Question.—Who were the Democrats that pulled and hauled and injured you on the day of election?

I know my boy came up and took hold of me to take me out of the crowd; Mr. Pumphrey also had hold of me, but there were so many I can't tell their names.

4th Question.—Did you not tell Captain Widdicombe on the day of election that you wanted to vote the Democratic ticket?

I do not know him; I do not remember of ever telling anybody so.

5th Question.—Did you or not see Mr. Brooke, the Contestant, a few days before the election, when you were housing tobacco at Mr. Pumphrey's, and tell him that you intended to vote for him?

I saw Mr. Brooke; I do not know him; I never exchanged a word with him; he came to the barn where Mr. Pumphrey was spearing tobacco.

6th Question.—Did you or not meet Mr. Wm. Pumphrey near Dr. Harper's on the day of election, and if yea, state what conversation you had with him?

Well, I met him there; he asked me if I had voted; I told

him no ; that people pulled and hauled me so I could not vote ; he said, "I have not voted yet," and got on his mare and came up toward the Court House, and I went on home.

7th Question.—Did Mr. Pumphrey get off his horse to hold this conversation with you, and did he request you to accompany him back to vote?

He had just come out of Mr. Harper's, and came to the post to get his horse ; he did not ask me to come back and vote.

8th Question.—Did you or not tell Mr. Pumphrey that he had better not go to the polls ; that if he did he might be killed?

No, sir ; to the question.

9th Question.—Have you ever told either of the Mr. Pumphreys, since the election, that you did not vote because you could not vote as you told him you were going to?

Yes, sir ; I have told that ; I would not vote for any man if I could not vote as I wanted to vote.

10th Question.—You say that you did not intend to come to the polls at all What induced you to change your mind?

I felt bad in the morning, and thought if I stayed at home. I would feel better, and fix my house. Mr. Pumphrey asked me to come to the house ; he called me to the house to get in the wagon to come to the election ; I told him I had no hat or jacket ; he gave me an old coat out of the house to slip on until I came back ; I then came down with him.

11th Question.—Did you have any conversation with Mr. Pumphrey about voting, on your way to the election, and if so, what was it?

I had no conversation with him ; did not exchange a word.

12th Question.—Did you have any conversation with Mr. Pumphrey upon any other subject on your way here?

I did not.

13th Question.—Did you tell either of the Mr. Pumphrey's on the day of election that you wanted to vote the Democratic ticket, and that you would go to Mr. Wilson's store, and wait until you could do so?

I never told him anything about such things.

Re-cross-examined :

1st Question.—You stated in your cross-examination that

you told Mr. Pumphrey that you would not vote at all if you could not vote as you desired. Please state if you did not wish to vote the Republican ticket; state further what was done with the coat Mr. Pumphrey gave you to come down.

It was my desire to vote the Republican ticket; I carried the coat back to Mr. Pumphrey.

ALEXANDER $\overset{\text{HIS}}{\underset{\text{MARK.}}{\times}}$ GROSS.

Test : RUFUS BELT.

DEPOSITION No. 10.

1st Question.—State your name, age, residence, occupation, and where you voted on the 4th day of November, 1873.

Name, S. G. Chaney; age, 43 years; residence, Seventh Election District, Prince George's County; occupation, farmer; I voted in Queen Anne District on the 4th of November, 1873.

2d Question.—Do you or do you not know of any non-residents who voted the Democratic ticket in the Seventh Election District or in Prince George's, at the election held on the 4th day of November, 1873? If yea, state all you know about it?

I know several that I do not consider residents of the district or county. Michael C. Sparrow—he has not been a resident of the county for three or four years; the last two years he has been in business in Baltimore and is still there. H. Brune Bowie—he also left the county some years ago; also in business in Baltimore; married and lives there with his family. Oden Mullikin also left the county some two years ago; his home was in Baltimore at the time of the election; he had some business in the Sun office. Walter W. W. Bowie—I don't consider him a resident of the county; he is in business in Baltimore, practicing law and editing the American Farmer. Arthur Mullikin left the county three or four years ago; went to Washington, and went into business there; he has changed his home several times since; never lived in Prince George's since he left.

3d Question.—Do you or do you not know Jacob Oakey, Oden Williams, Charles Stewart and Elsey Tilghman, and did they vote in the Seventh Election District on the day of election, and was there any intimidation used to prevent their voting the Democratic ticket?

I know Elsey Tilghman and Jacob Oakey. Tilghman voted, Oakey did not; so they say. No intimidation that I know of.

4th Question.—Did you or did you not see Democratic tickets in the hands of Republican voters, marked "True Blue?" If so, do you know by whom they were marked; why they were marked, and were any of such taken from the ballot-box and counted by the Judges?

I did see tickets in the hands of the Republicans, marked "True Blue." Richard Peach marked the tickets; he was a Judge of the Election. I do not know why they were marked, but judge that it would enable him to see if they were voted; there was one so marked, taken from the ballot-box and counted.

5th Question.—Was not said Richard Peach a Democratic Judge of election, a warm supporter of Brooke, the Contestant, and state how you know these tickets were so marked?

He was a Democratic Judge and a warm supporter of Brooke; I was at Mitchelsville the morning of the election, to a breakfast given by the Republicans, and Elsey Tilghman came to me and said he had a Democratic ticket given to him by Richard Peach; that he did not wish to vote it, and gave me the ticket and requested me to give him a Republican ticket; that Democratic ticket was marked "True Blue." I asked him how he came by that ticket, and then I asked him why Peach gave him that ticket; he said that he was old and poor, and Mr. Peach had promised him meal and meat. He voted the Republican ticket, that being the ticket he desired to vote.

6th Question.—State, if you please, if you were or were not, during the most of the day of 4th of November, 1873, at or near the polls in the Seventh District? If so, was there not free access to the polls to all desiring to vote who were qualified? Did you hear threats or intimidation to prevent voters from voting their true sentiments, and was not the result a fair expression of the sentiments of the legally qualified voters of the Seventh District?

I was at or near the polls from about 10 o'clock A. M. until the tickets were counted; there was free access to all who desired to vote. I heard no threats or intimidation used. The result was a fair expression of the sentiment of the people.

Cross-examination :

1st Question.—Did you see each of the parties that you consider non-residents vote at said election; did you see their tickets, and do you know positively that each and all of them voted the entire Democratic ticket without a scratch?

No ; to the question.

2d Question.—Do you know if either of these parties have ever voted or applied to register or vote elsewhere than in Prince George's County?

I do not know.

3d Question.—State, if you please, how long each of said parties have been voting in Prince George's County?

Sparrow has been voting there at intervals for five or six years, or longer ; Brune Bowie has been voting there since he was 21 ; Oden Mullikin has been doing the same, I think ; Walter W. Bowie has been voting there for twenty-two years, I know ; Arthur Mullikin has been voting there, at different times, ever since he has been a voter.

4th Question.—Do you know if either of said parties ever abandoned their residence in this county and sought to acquire one elsewhere?

I don't know ; Col. W. W. W. Bowie moved his family to Baltimore ; Brune Bowie married in Baltimore, and lives there with his family ; the others had no families.

5th Question.—Please state if you have ever heard either of these parties declare their intention to retain their residence in this county?

I have ; I heard Oden Mullikin say that he was going West, to make his home there ; he is the only one I have heard say to the contrary ; have spoken to some of the others about voting here, and they said they always had voted here, and would continue to.

6th Question.—Do you know when the ticket marked " True Blue " was given to Elsey Tilghman?

I heard Richard Peach say that he gave Elsey Tilghman and James Oakey their tickets the day before the election, at Governor's Bridge.

7th Question.—Did Tilghman say that he had promised to vote said ticket?

9

He did not say whether he had promised or not, but I judge he did, or he would not have had it.

8th Question.—Did he state how Mr. Peach came to promise him meal and meat, or what conversation occurred between him and Mr. Peach on the subject?

He did not state to me how Mr. Peach came to promise him meal and meat ; he showed me the ticket, and I judged from his having the ticket that Mr. Peach had promised to give him meal and meat if he would vote it ; he said he was old and feeble, and not able to work much.

9th Question.—Did you use any argument or offer any inducement to the said Tilghman to vote the Republican ticket, or was the conversation you had with him commenced by Tilghman, and in what manner?

Tilghman called me aside and said he had something to show me. He pulled the Democratic ticket out of his pocket ; he said he did not wish to vote it ; he handed the ticket to me and requested me to give him a Republican ticket. I used no argument nor offered any inducement.

10th Question.—Did you or not see any Democratic tickets, or Republican tickets with the names of Democratic candidates upon them, taken from colored voters on the day of election, torn up or retained, and Republican tickets given in their stead?

I did not.

11th Question.—Did you not state to one of the Judges of Election that you had taken Democratic tickets away from voters that said Judge had given to them, destroyed the same, given the parties Republican tickets in their stead, and that they voted the same?

I never told any one so.

12th Question.—Do you know John Hawkins, Spencer Lee, Frank Sprigg and his son ; if you know either, please state where they live with their families, and how long they have lived at their present abode?

I know Hawkins ; he is living at George Mitchel's place now ; has lived there since the first of January ; he lived at John Peach's at the time of the election ; don't know where he lived prior to that. I know Spencer Lee ; do not know where he lives ; whether in said county or Washington. I know Frank Sprigg ; don't know his son ; don't know where Frank Sprigg or his family live.

13th Question.—Did you see either of these parties on the day of election, and do you know if they voted in the county, and how they, or either of them, voted?

I recollect seeing Hawkins, but none others; I don't know if he voted or how he voted, but judge he voted.

Re-cross-examined :

1st Question.—State, if you please, why you believe the parties you consider non-residents voted the Democratic ticket, and do you think any particular notice would have been taken of their voting but for the attempt of Mr. Brooke, the Contestant, to dispute the vote of Republican voters whose cases are strictly parallel with the parties named?

I believe they voted the Democratic ticket because they advocated the cause of Democracy, and Mr. Brooke in particular ; I do not think there would have been any notice taken but for the attempt of Mr. Brooke to dispute the rights.

Re-examined by the Contestant :

1st Question.—You state that these parties, whom you considered non-residents, were advocating the Democratic cause and Mr. Brooke in particular? Now state, if you please, if they were advocating the claims of any of the other candidates upon the Democratic ticket with equal earnestness?

I don't think they did.

2d Question.—Had not one of them a brother and the other a son on said Democratic ticket? If so, which of them?

W. W. W. Bowie had a son on the ticket and Brune Bowie had a brother ; but I don't think they were particular about him ; he had a son in office.

S. G. CHANEY.

Test: RUFUS BELT.

DEPOSITION No. 11.

1st Question.—State your name, age, residence, occupation, and where you voted on the 4th day of November, 1873.

Name, Philip Jones ; age, 48 years ; reside in Nottingham District ; occupation, laborer ; voted in Nottingham District.

2d Question.—Do you know Ambrose and Hamilton Carroll, and how long have you known them, and do you or not know if they were born prior to the killing of Crook by Dr. Worthington?

I do know them; I have known them since they were two days old; they were born before the killing of Mr. Crook.

Cross-examined:

1st Question.—When did the killing of Crook by Worthington occur?

I do not know the date, but it was done in the fall.

2d Question.—Can you read and write?

No, sir.

3d Question.—By what means do you fix the date of birth of these parties?

From my recollection; they were born in January; at the time I was serving at Mr. Burch's; he gave me a bundle to carry down to Robert Carroll, the father of those children, Ambrose and Hamilton, his children; he gave me a message to carry to Robert Carroll to take care of those children, and let nothing happen until Dr. Skinner could get home; I am satisfied that Mr. Crook was not dead; I was talking with Carroll; Mr. Hook came up; asked me what I was talking about; I went on to tell him, and he said he would have me to know that he was Dr. Skinner in the Doctor's absence; Mr. Hook got after me with a cart-pin, and Mr. Crook said he ought not to do so.

4th Question.—Do you know what year this was?

I do not know.

Re-cross-examined:

1st Question.—You state in your testimony-in-chief that you know that Ambrose and Hamilton Carroll were born prior to the killing of Mr. Crook by Dr. Worthington, because Dr. Skinner had gone to New Orleans to transact certain business, and that he had left Mr. Hook in charge of his plantation during his absence; and during this period there was a difficulty between Mr. Hook and Crook, and that Mr. Crook, then being alive, interposed, to prevent Mr. Hook from taking any undue advantage; and you further know that at this time, Mr. Crook being still alive, that these boys, Ambrose and Hamilton Carroll, were then in existence?

[The above question withdrawn by the Defendant.]

2d Question.—You stated in your testimony-in-chief that

Ambrose and Hamilton Carroll were born in the absence of Dr. Skinner, and when you went to carry this bundle to Carroll and these two boys—and this difficulty took place between Hook and yourself; Crook, who was living at that time, took your part, and these children were in existence at that time? Please state, if you know, where Dr. Skinner had gone?

That these children were in existence, and Dr. Skinner had gone to New Orleans.

Re-cross-examination :

1st Question.—How do you know that Dr. Skinner had gone to New Orleans, and what year was it?

I don't know what year it was. Mr. Burch told me he had gone to New Orleans.

PHILIP ⋈ JONES.
HIS
MARK.

Test : RUFUS BELT.

DEPOSITION No. 12.

1st Question.—State your name, age, residence, occupation, and where you voted on the 4th day of November, 1873?

My name is Robert Carroll ; age, 52, the 14th of February ; live in Nottingham District ; occupation, farmer ; I voted in Nottingham District.

2d Question.—Are you the father of Ambrose and Hamilton Carroll, and were they born prior to the killing of Crook by Dr. Worthington?

Yes, sir ; to the question.

3d Question.—Did any one try to intimidate these boys from voting by telling them that if they voted they would be presented to the Grand Jury ; and did you say to any one that you did not believe that these boys were old enough to vote?

Mr. Jesse Ryon told them on election day that if they voted what would be the consequence ; he did not tell what—though the boys were of age. I did not tell any one that they were not old enough to vote.

4th Question.—Will you state if Ambrose and Hamilton Carroll were not 21 years of age on the 4th day of November, 1873, and legally qualified voters?

Yes, sir ; they were going on 22 years ; they were legally qualified.

Cross-examination :

1st Question.—Can you read and write, and did you make any record of the birth of these children?

I can read, but cannot write. I did not make any record, but I know precisely what day and month they were born; they were born on the 10th of January, but I do not know the year.

2d Question.—Did you go with these parties to secure their registration, and by what data did you fix the time of their birth, before the Register?

I went with them to get registered; I told the Register that I was satisfied of their age by the fact that Dr. Skinner was in New Orleans, and Dr. Worthington attended my family— Skinner having employed Worthington in his absence.

3d Question.—Did you not also tell Mr. Coffren, or any one else, that these children were born while Dr. Skinner was away, from some cause in connection with the killing of Crook by Worthington, or words to that effect?

Yes, sir.

4th Question.—Are you positive now that Dr. Worthington attended your wife in confinement with these children, and do you know it of your own knowledge, or have you obtained the impression from others?

I am confident of that; I know it of my own knowledge; I did not get the impression from others.

5th Question.—Have you not been hiring these boys out, and collecting their wages as minors, and up to what time have you done so?

I have been hiring them out, and collecting their wages. One of them I hired to Mr. Coffren for the whole year of 1873; he stayed there for the year; also, hired the other one to Mr. Coffren for the year 1873, but he left at Easter; then he hired himself to Mrs. Lelly. I collected the wages of Ambrose for the whole of last year, but Hamilton's I did not. I did not collect it, because he was not a man; as he was obedient, I collected it and gave it to him.

6th Question.—Did you or your wife go to Mr. Coffren a few days before the election, and tell him that you were satisfied that these boys were not of age, and asked to have their names stricken from the registration list?

No, sir ; neither of us said a word to him.

7th Question.—Do you know whether the boys went to him with any such statement, or either of them ?

He tried to frighten the boy by making threats, saying he would be put in jail or penitentiary ; the boy then said if that was the case, to strike his name off; the boy came home and told me, and I told him he was wrong. I asked him what he did it for, and he said, "Father, Mr. Coffren kept bothering me so."

8th Question.—Where are these boys living now ?

They are living with me in the county.

9th Question.—You say that you told Mr. Coffren that these children were born while Dr. Skinner was away from home, in connection with the killing of Crook by Worthington. Please state when that occurred, giving the year.

I do not know the year Worthington killed Crook.

10th Question.—Did you hear any threats or intimidation used by any one towards these boys, or either of them, with reference to their right to vote? If so, state by whom the threats were made, the character of them, and all about it.

None at all, except by Mr. Ryon ; he did did not say anything, but to Ambrose ; tried to prevent him from voting. Ambrose said he was of age, and he would vote. Then Mr. Ryon told him that if he would vote, he would put him to some difficulty. Ambrose did vote.

11th Question.—How close were you to Mr. Ryon when he said this, and how far from the polls did this conversation occur ?

All together ; close by the window where the election took place.

12th Question.—Did these boys vote, and do you know how they voted ?

They both voted the Republican ticket.

ROBERT ^{HIS} CARROLL.
MARK.

Test : RUFUS BELT.

DEPOSITION No. 13.

1st Question.—State your name, age, residence, occupation, and where you voted on the 4th day of November, 1873.

My name is Benjamin Fletcher, Sr.; age, 56 years the 15th of last month; residence, Queen Anne District; occupation, farmer; I voted in Queen Anne District on the 4th of November, 1873.

2d Question.—Do you know a man named Jacob Oakey; whether or not he voted on 4th of November; how he voted; if he voted, and any circumstances connected with his voting?

I know Oakey; he told me that he did not vote on the day of election; he said that he had always voted the Republican ticket, and wanted to continue, but that Mr. Richard Peach promised to give him two bushels of meal if he would vote the Democratic ticket open at the window, so that he could see it. He said he intended to vote his own ticket, if he could get it in without Mr. Peach seeing him.

3d Question.—Do you know Elsey Tilghman? If so, state if he voted under the influence of violence or not, or anything you may know connected with his voting.

I know Elsey Tilghman; I do not know how he voted; at breakfast he brought me a Democratic ticket which he said Mr. Peach gave him; he asked me for a ticket, said he wanted to vote his own ticket; I told him if he had promised Mr. Peach to vote the Democratic ticket, he was privileged to do so; he said he had not promised to do so; then I referred him to Mr. Chaney to get a ticket.

4th Question.—Do you know of any non-residents who voted at the election on the 4th day of November, held in Prince George's County, and voted the Democratic ticket?

I know of Chas. Contee, a colored man, whose family reside in Washington, whose vote has always been objected to until this, when he turned a Democrat; and was registered Chas. Contee; had always lived at Mr. Walker's in this county.

Cross-examined:

1st Question.—Do you know if Jacob Oakey and Elsey Tilghman are now residing in Prince George's County, and at the time of election; and if they have removed from it since?

They both lived in Prince George's County at the time of voting, and they both still live there.

2d Question.—Did you use any persuasion or offer any inducements to Elsey Tilghman, to vote the Republican ticket; and do you know if he did vote the Republican ticket?

Did not use any persuasion; offered no inducements; because I did not think it necessary; I do not know how he voted.

3d Question.—Do you know of any non-residents of the county or State, who voted the Republican ticket in Prince George's, at said election.

[Objections filed to the above question, on the ground not responsive to any question asked upon the examination-in-chief].

I do not know.

4th Question.—Do you or not know John Hawkins, Frank Sprigg and son, who formerly lived with F. M. Hall and Spencer Lee. If yea, state where they lived prior to, and at the date of the late election; where their families lived; if they voted in Queen Anne's, and how they voted?

[Objected to upon the ground that it is not connected with, or in any way responsive to the questions asked at the examination-in-chief.]

I know John Hawkins; his mother and father were living at Mr. Peach's at the time of the election; John Hawkins had been living there with them for three years, up to after harvest; went to Washington and stayed until a week before the election; has been staying in the county ever since; he voted in Queen Anne's; I gave him a Republican ticket; don't know how he voted; I know Frank Spriggs; I do not know his son; I do not know where he lived; think he lived at Mr. Berry's; I think he was registered in Queen Anne's, but do not know if he voted there this fall; did not see him on the day of election. I know Spencer Lee; he had been living with Mr. Mullikin up to harvest; he has no family; his father lives in Washington; he went to Washington after harvest and came back two weeks before the election; I gave him a Republican ticket; I believe he voted, but don't know how he voted.

5th Question.—Do you know positively how Charles Contee voted?

I know only what he told me, that he wanted to vote for Mr. Frederick Duvall.

BENJAMIN ☒ FLETCHER.
HIS
MARK.

Test: RUFUS BELT.

DEPOSITION No. 14.

1st Question.—State your name, age, residence, occupation, and where you voted on the 4th day of November, 1873.

My name is Francis Allen; age, 28 years; occupation, laborer; residence, Prince George's County, Md.; I voted in the Ninth Election District on the 4th of November, 1873.

2d Question.—State where you now reside, and where you have resided for the last several years; how long you have resided where you now live; if your residence there is permanent, and where you have been voting?

I reside in Washington; I have resided, for the last several years, in Surratt's District, Prince George's County; ten months in Washington; my residence there is not permanent; I intend to return to Prince George's County; I have been voting in Surratt's District, and have never voted elsewhere.

Cross-examined:

1st Question.—Will you please state if you have ever applied for registration or voted elsewhere, but in Prince George's County, and how you voted at the late election?

[The above question objected to; the objection sustained by the Justice, that it did not relate to the testimony-in-chief; to which ruling, Mr. Brooke's counsel excepted].

2d Question.—You state in your examination-in-chief that you have been in Washington for ten months; please say when you went to Washington, and where you went from?

I went to Washington April 14th, 1873; I went from Prince George's County, Surratt's District.

3d Question.—Will you please state how you voted at the late election, if a Democratic ticket or Republican ticket?

[Counsel for R. S. Widdicombe objected to the above, on the ground that it was a leading question; the ballot being a secret matter, he was not bound to answer. The Justice ruled, that it was not pertinent to any of the examination-in-chief, and sustained the objection; refused to let the witness answer, from which ruling the counsel excepted.]

4th Question.—Please state in what Legislative District of Washington City you lived, during the aforesaid ten months referred to by you.

The Twenty-second District, I think ; I am not acquainted with the districts.

5th Question.—Where were you living on the 16th of September, 1873 ?

In Washington City.

6th Question.—Do you or do you not know if there was a registration of voters on the 16th day of September, 1873, in Washington City?

I do not.

7th Question.—Are you a married man or not ; if married, please state where your family resided on the day of election, the 4th of November, 1873?

I am a married man ; a part of my family reside in Washington, and a part in Prince George's County, Surratt's District.

8th Question.—Please state what part of your family resided in Washington on the 4th day of November, 1873 ?

My wife ; no one else.

9th Question.—Please state what you mean when you say, I intend to return to Prince George's County ?

I mean to make Prince George's County my place of residence, of course.

10th Question.—Do you intend to make Prince George's County your residence from this time forward, or from what time ?

I have not yet decided upon what time I will move to Prince George's County ; I have always claimed my residence here ; do not know at what time I intend to date my residence there.

11th Question.—Please state how many times you have voted in Surratt's District, and how many years you have been in said district ?

I do not know how often I have voted there. I have resided there since 1845 ; I was born there.

12th Question.—What do you mean to say when you say your residence in Washington is not permanent?

I mean that my employment there is temporary.

13th Question.—Is it your intention to make Prince George's County your place of residence, although you have stated that your residence in Washington was temporary, and not permanent?

It is my intention.

14th *Question.*—What was your occupation on the day of election, immediately preceding it, and since that time; and if engaged in business at this time, what is it, and where do you carry it on?

My occupation was a laborer in the United States Navy Yard, at Washington; I was there before the election, and I am still employed there.

15th *Question.*—Where did you have your washing done on the day of election, previous to that day, and to the present time?

In the month of September I had my washing done in Surratt's District; since then I have had it done in Washington.

16th *Question.*—When was the last time you had any occupation in Prince George's County, where was the same, and what was the particular occupation engaged in?

The last time I was employed in Prince George's County was on the 4th of July, 1873, in Spalding's District; a confectioner.

17th *Question.*—What was the occasion of your acting as confectioner, on the 4th of July, 1873; were you doing business for yourself, or for some one else?

[Objected to by Mr. Merrick on the ground of irrelevancy and immateriality; objection sustained; exceptions to the ruling.]

18th *Question.*—Did you own any real or personal estate property before the day of election, on the day of election, or since that time, in Prince George's County?

I owned personal property previous to the election; that is, before I went to Washington; I did not own any on the day of election, nor since that time. I have not owned real estate since 1872; I think I disposed of it in July or August, 1872.

19th *Question.*—Has your family ever resided in the Ninth Election District of said County, and if so, for what period of time, and during said residence whether house-keeping, boarding, or visiting?

Yes; they have resided there; don't know how long; part of the time visiting and a part boarding; they were not housekeeping. In 1870 I resided there, and kept house; also in 1868 and part of 1867.

20th Question.—How long was your family boarding in said district, and how long visiting ?

I don't know.

21st Question.—Did you ever pay any money for boarding your family in said district; if yea, how much did you pay, and to whom did you pay it ?

[Objected to by Mr. Gwynn ; ruling by the Justice, that so much of the question as pertains to paying any money for board, admitted ; refusal to allow the last part of the question to be answered ; excepted to by the counsel for Brooke ; exception by Mr. Gwynn to the ruling in allowing any portion to be answered.]   .

I have paid money for boarding.

Cross-examined :

1st Question.—Did you ever consider that you had any residence other than that in Prince George's County, and was not your stay in Washington temporary, and for the purpose of getting work?

I did not.   It was temporary.

FRANCIS ALLEN.

Test :   RUFUS BELT.

DEPOSITION No. 15.

1st Question.—State your name, age, residence, occupation, and where you voted on the 4th day of November, 1873.

Name, John McNelly ; 38 years last November ; residence, Prince George's County ; occupation, copper roller ; voted in the Ninth Election District, Surratt's.

Cross-examined :

1st Question—How long, prior to the election, had you re-sided in the Ninth Election District?

[The above question allowed and consented to after objection.]

I keep no memoranda ; I have resided and voted in Surratt's District for four years ; I moved to Washington and back during that time twice ; Surratt's District is my residence.

2d Question.—Have you or not, during the said four years, ever voted in Washington City?

I have not.

3d Question.—Do you or not own the homestead upon which

you reside in this county? And, if not, to whom does the same belong?

I do not own the same; it belongs to Mrs. Julia Murphy, my wife's mother.

4th Question.—Where do you carry on the business of copper roller?

I am working for the United States Government at Washington Navy Yard.

5th Question.—How did you vote on the day of election?

[Objected to by Mr. Merrick, upon the ground that it is not responsive or in any way connected with the examination-in-chief. Objection sustained by the Justice. Exception noted by counsel for Mr. Brooke.]

6th Question.—Have you, during the said four years, resided with your family in Washington City?

I have.

7th Question.—When and for what time?

I do not know the dates; I have not resided there longer than nine months at any time; moved there in the fall, moved back in the spring.

8th Question.—How long prior to the election did you move from Washington City to this county, and how long had you been residing in Washington City prior to said move?

At the time of the election I was living in Washington City temporarily, where I had been residing eight or nine months temporarily.

9th Question.—Have you moved to this county since the election?

I have not.

JOHN McNELLY.

Test : Rufus Belt.

Deposition No. 16.

1st Question.—State your name, age, occupation, residence, and where you voted on the 4th day of November, 1873.

Name, John Ridout; age, 54 years; occupation, laborer; residence, Queen Anne District; voted in the Seventh District on the 4th day of November, 1873.

2d Question.—Do you know James Oakey, Oden Williams, Charles Stewart, Elsey Tilghman, or either of them, and if they, or either of them, were prevented from voting the Democratic ticket on said day, as they wished to vote on the 4th of November, 1873, at the election held on the 4th of November, 1873?

[Objection by Mr. Roberts, counsel for Contestant, on the ground that it is secondary evidence. Objection overruled. Exceptions noticed by Mr. Roberts, counsel for Contestant. Further objection by the counsel for Contestant, that it was James Oakey, and not Jacob Oakey, in the notice. Objection to Tilghman on the ground that the notice served on Henry Brooke does not contain the name of Elsey Tilghman. Objection made by Mr. Roberts. Objections sustained.]

I do not know James Oakey. I know Oden Williams and Charles Stewart; they were not prevented from voting the Democratic ticket. I gave Oden Williams, at his request, a Republican ticket, and he said he wished to vote it; I saw a Republican ticket given to Charles Stewart by Benjamin Fletcher. I heard him tell Fletcher he wanted to vote it.

Cross-examination:

1st Question.—Can you read?

No, sir.

2d Question.—Did you or not ask Oden Williams to vote the Republican ticket?

No, sir.

3d Question.—How did you know the ticket given to Charles Stewart was a Republican ticket?

Because Mr. Chaney gave it to Benjamin Fletcher, Jr., at Mitchelsville; and Benjamin Fletcher, Jr., gave it to Charles Stewart. He knew the Republican ticket because it had a head on it.

4th Question.—Do you or not know whose names were written on said ticket voted by Charles Stewart?

Yes, sir.

5th Question.—Did you vote the Democratic or Republican ticket on the day of election?

[Objected to, by Mr. Merrick, that it has no connection or responsive to the examination-in-chief. Objection sustained by the Justice. Exception to the ruling of the Justice by Mr. Roberts, counsel.]

6th Question.—How do you know that the ticket given at Mitchelsville, by Mr. Chaney to Benjamin Fletcher, Jr., was the same ticket given by said Fletcher to Charles Stewart at Queen Anne's?

Samuel Jennings, who could read, examined the ticket that Fletcher had, and he said it was a Republican ticket.

JOHN ᴴᴵˢ ⋈ RIDOUT.
ᴹᴬᴿᴷ.

Test: Rufus Belt.

Deposition No. 17.

1st Question.—State your name, age, residence, occupation, and where you voted on the 4th of November, 1873?

Name, Oden Williams; I don't know my age exactly; my mistress told me I was 22 years up to election day; occupation, laborer; Queen Anne District; I voted in Queen Anne District.

2d Question.—Where you forced or not to vote the Republican ticket on the day of election? State any conversation you had with Mr. John Earnshaw in reference to said voting, and all about it.

I was not forced to vote the Republican ticket; I did it voluntarily. Mr. Earnshaw asked me to vote the Democratic ticket, and said he would pay me; I told him I did not want to vote the Democratic ticket—it was my first vote and I wanted to vote the Republican ticket.

Cross-examination:

1st Question.—Did you or not tell Mr. Earnshaw, before the election, that you wished and intended to vote the Democratic ticket and for Mr. Brooke?

No, sir. I did not.

2d Question.—By whom were you asked to vote the Republican ticket?

By no one. I voted my own sentiments.

3d Question.—Can you read?

I cannot.

ODEN ᴴᴵˢ ⋈ WILLIAMS.
ᴹᴬᴿᴷ.

Test: Rufus Belt.

DEPOSITION No. 18.

1st Question.—State your name, age, residence, occupation, and where you voted on the 4th day of November, 1873.

[Objections by Mr. Roberts, counsel for Mr. Brooke, upon the ground that the name of Benjamin I. Gwynn does not appear upon the list furnished by R. S. Widdicombe to Henry Brooke, his name being Benedict I., and not Benjamin I. Gwynn. Objection overruled by the Justice on the ground that it contained the name of Benjamin I. Gwynn, which was clear that it was the man wanted, without a misnomer.]

My name is Benedict I. Gwynn; I always write it B. I. Gwynn; age, 54 years; residence, Piscataway District; occupation, attorney-at-law; voted in the Fifth Election District on the 4th of November, 1873.

2d Question.—Were you in the Fifth Election District on the 4th of November last? State, if you please, if any one was prevented from voting there by threats or intimidation, and what was the condition of things at the polls on that day.

I was there on that day from about 9½ o'clock until the polls closed, and no one, to my knowledge, was prevented from voting, through fears, threats, or intimidation. There was the excitement incidental to all elections only. The election progressed as quietly and as orderly as usual; there seemed to be a fair expression of sentiment generally, and the result of the election was a fair expression of the people of that district, and no voter had reason to fear for his personal safety, by any demonstrations or other conduct on the part of those present. I did not absent myself from the polls on the day of election twenty minutes at any one time, or one hour altogether, and know there was ample time for every person desiring to vote to do so, without hindrance, interference, or obstruction; there were several hours in the afternoon when the way to the polls was entirely unobstructed by any crowd or persons, and there was free access to the polls. I saw three strange colored men, said to be from Uniontown, who had oysters for sale, and who went around and talked quietly to their colored friends, but who did not interfere with the rights of anybody. I saw no violence attempted, and the election passed off more quietly than most elections I have attended

10

in Piscataway; the quietness and fairness of the election was a subject of universal remark.

Cross-examined:

1st Question.—Were you at the place of voting during the whole day, and could you have seen or been cognizant of all illegal voting, had there been any such?

I was present from $9\frac{1}{2}$ o'clock until the closing of these polls, with very short absences; it was impossible for me to be cognizant of all illegal voting, if any.

2d Question.—Did not the colored voters exclusively occupy the front door approaching the polls, during the early part of the day, and were not non-residents, both white and colored, at said polls, endeavoring to influence the colored vote in favor of the Republican ticket?

In the early part of the morning there were crowds of both white and colored voters in front of the polls, awaiting their turn to vote, who, so soon as they voted, fell back and let others come up. I saw no one, whether residents or non-residents, attempting to improperly influence colored voters to vote the Republican ticket. I saw General Walker there during the day; I do not know where he resides, but have heard in Washington. I was often with him during the day, and he in no wise interfered with voters during the election.

3d Question.—Are you not acting as the attorney for Mr. Widdicombe in the matter of this contest?

I am neither employed, or acting as attorney for Mr. Widdicombe, but as his friend.

4th Question.—What ticket did you vote on the day of election?

[Objected to on the ground that it is not connected with, or responsive to any question as to the examination-in-chief; objection sustained; exceptions noted by Mr. Roberts, counsel for Contestant.]

B. I. GWYNN.

Test: RUFUS BELT.

DEPOSITION No. 19.

1st Question.—State your name, age, residence, occupation, and where you voted on the 4th day of November, 1873.

My name is Charles Marshall; age, 28 years; residence,

Prince George's County; occupation, laborer; I voted in Marlboro' District.

2d Question.—State where you are residing now, and how long you have been there, and what induced you to go there, and if you intend to remain permanently where you now are?

I am now in Washington; I went there last November a year; returned in March; stayed in Washington ten months; I have no family; I was induced to go to Washington to get work; I did not intend making Washington my home.

3d Question.—Do you know Wm. Orme and Samuel Williams, and where their home is?

Yes, I know them; Wm. Orme is living with me; he went away from Prince George's in July; Samuel Williams claims his home here, so he says.

4th Question.—Where do you keep your clothes, and since when?

I have been keeping them in Washington since March, 1873.

Cross-examined:

1st Question.—Where are you living now?

I am living in Washington.

2d Question.—Where is Wm. Orme now?

In Washington.

3d Question.—Did not Wm. Orme leave W. B. Hill's place in this county about two years ago, and go to Washington to live?

No, sir, he did not.

4th Question.—When did he leave Mr. Hill's?

He left W. B. Hill's year before last, and went to work on the railroad.

5th Question.—When you came back from Washington in March, 1873, where did you reside, and what occupation did you follow while here?

I was visiting about here, and worked some on the railroad in Charles County.

6th Question.—Why did you come back from Washington in March?

Because work was scarce in Washington; I came down to see my mother and get work here.

7th Question.—How often have you voted in Washington? I have never voted in Washington.

CHAS. ⋈ MARSHALL.
HIS   MARK.

Test: Rufus Belt.

Deposition No. 20.

EXHIBIT—GEO. LOCKER.

Circuit Court for Prince George's County,—April Term, 1868.

State of Maryland vs. *George Locker, negro.*—Presentment and indictment for larceny, 1868, April 20th. Prisoner arraigned and pleads not guilty. Guilty. 1868, April 28th, sentenced to Penitentiary for one (1) year.

State of Maryland, Prince George's County, Sct:

I hereby certify, That the aforegoing .is truly taken and copied from the Minutes and Proceedings of the Circuit Court for Prince George's County, at the April Term, 1868, thereof; and that it does not appear from any entry therein, that the said George Locker has been pardoned, or his sentence in any manner commuted.

In testimony whereof, I hereunto subscribe my name and affix the seal of the Circuit Court for Prince [SEAL.] George's County, this 23d day of January, Anno Domini, 1874.

HENRY BROOKE,

Clerk of the Circuit Court for Prince George's County, Md.

1st Question.—State your name, age, residence, occupation, and where you voted on the 4th day of November, 1873.

George Locker; 40 years old; residence, Prince George's County, Ninth District; occupation, farmer; voted in the Ninth District.

2d Question.—Were you ever tried and convicted for larceny and sentenced to the Penitentiary; and if so, state when it was; and did you serve out your time?

I was tried and convicted, and sent to the Penitentiary in 1868; served my time out, and came back 1869.

3d Question.—State how you voted; if you voted the Republican ticket or the Democratic ticket?

I voted the square Republican ticket.

4th Question.—State if any efforts were made to induce you to vote the Democratic ticket; and, if so, by whom, and what efforts were?

As to the efforts, Mr. Jarboe came down before the nomination; told me if I helped him he would help me; he said nothing about voting; Judge Wilson gave me three dollars; Henry Brooke gave me two dollars; Charles Stanley one dollar. They said nothing about voting; said, help us.

5th Question.—What did the parties mean by helping us?

They meant, vote for us; they asked me how many men I could get to vote for them; I told them about twenty-five to help them.

6th Question.—At the time of your return from the penitentiary, had colored men the right to vote in this county?

No, sir; not for two years after.

7th Question.—How often have you voted?

Twice; first vote, two years ago.

Cross-examination:

1st Question.—Do you own any land?

No, sir.

2d Question.—Hav you ever been pardoned by the Governor of the State?

No, sir.

3d Question.—Did you register and vote the first year colored people were allowed to vote in this State?

No, sir.

4th Question.—Did not Mr. Henry Brooke give you two dollars for bringing his horse to Marlboro', at the time referred to by you in your examination-in-chief?

No, sir.

5th Question.—Did you not bring Mr. Brooke's horse to Marlboro' on that day, and from what place?

No, sir.

6th Question.—Did you not tell Mr. Wilson that at the time he gave you the three dollars, that there were some men you could get to vote for him, and asked him to give you some money to assist in electioneering for him?

Yes, sir; I did. I told him I could get twenty-five men.

7th Question.—Was or not the two dollars given you by Mr.

Brooke, and the dollar by Mr. Stanley, to assist you in recovering your horse lost in Marlboro' on the night you were here.

No, sir.   They gave me this money before I lost the horse.

GEORGE ^{HIS} ⋈ LOCKER.

MARK.

Test: RUFUS BELT.

DEPOSITION No. 21.

1st Question.—State your name, age, residence, occupation, and where you voted on the 4th of November, 1873.

Benjamin F. Duvall ; age, 42 years ; residence, Marlboro' District ; occupation, farmer ; I voted in the Third Election District, Prince George's County.

2d Question.—Do you know Alexander Gross, Sr., and do you know how he desired to vote on the 4th day of November, 1873 ?

I do know Gross ; I saw him several times during the campaign ; always told me that he intended to vote the Republican ticket and no other.   I heard him tell Mr. McCullough that he wanted to vote the Republican ticket.

3d Question.—Do you know Joe Gallaway and how he desired to vote on the 4th of November, 1873 ?

I have known Joe Gallaway all my life ; I saw him often during the campaign ; he promised me all the time to vote the Republican ticket.

4th Question.—Do you know Aquilla Wilson, John T. Low, Daniel Clark, George Hammond, Robert Oliver, J. S. Higgins, John Buckmaster, Joseph Wikers, Michael Sparrow, H. Brune Bowie, Oden Mullikin, John F. Mudd, W. W. W. Bowie, Carter Hall, C. C. Hyatt, Jr., or either of them ; if yea, state which of them you know, where they resided on the 4th of November, 1873 ; where they voted on that day, and for whom they voted ?

I know Aquilla Wilson ; he lives in Baltimore ; voted in Marlboro'; do not know how he voted ; he has lived in Baltimore two or three years, I believe ; I don't know exactly.   I know Mr. Lowe ; he has lived in Baltimore three years, I know ; he voted in Upper Marlboro'; I don't know that he voted.   I know Mr. Clark ; he has been living in Baltimore or Washington for the last four or five years ; he voted in Upper

Marlboro'; I suppose he voted the Democratic ticket, as he was a Democratic candidate. George Hammond, Robert Oliver and J. Lack Higgins, I don't know. I know John Buckmaster; he has been living in Washington for eighteen months; he told me he voted the Democratic ticket, with the exception of Mr. Suit. I know Joseph Wikers; he used to be a conductor on the cars; he does not reside in this county; he voted in Marlboro'; he showed me his ticket—it was a full Democratic ticket, with the exception of my name. I know Michael Sparrow; he lives, I suppose, in Baltimore, if anywhere; I do not know if he voted. Mr. W. W. W. Bowie lives in Baltimore; I do not know if he voted; he invited me to his house. I know nothing about the rest—where they live or how they voted.

5th Question.—Was or was not the election held on the 4th of November, in Marlboro' District, fairly conducted?

It was as fair an election as ever I saw held here; everybody got every vote they could.

Cross-examined:

1st Question.—Do you know how Alec Gross, Sr., voted?

I do not know how he voted; I do not know that he did vote.

2d Question.—Did Joseph Gallaway promise you on the day of election to vote the Republican ticket?

He did not.

3d Question.—You have stated you were a farmer; are you not also a member of the Commissioners of Court, and elected to that office on the Republican ticket in November, 1873?

I am a member of the Commissioners of Court; was upon the Republican ticket.

4th Question.—How do you know that Aquilla Wilson resides in Baltimore City, or how long he has been there; his character of residence, if temporary or permanent, and his occupation there, if any?

He told me he lived in Baltimore; gave me the number of his house; said he was a plasterer; if I heard of any jobs in the county to let him know; he would be glad to get them; I have seen him there frequently for two or three years; I cannot say if his residence is temporary or permanent.

5th Question.—Has not Aquilla Wilson always voted in this county?

I do not know; I know that he voted here the last election.

6th Question.—Is not John T. Lowe temporarily employed in the Tobacco Warehouse in Baltimore, and has he not always voted in this county?

No, sir; he is not nor has been in the warehouse for twelve months; he works for Dipe, Hill & Co.; he has always voted in this county.

7th Question.—Has not Mr. Clark a law office in Marlboro'; does he not practice law in this county, and has he not always voted in this county?

He has an office here; he practices law here; he has always voted in Queen Anne's District, in this county; until this fall he voted in Marlboro'.

8th Question.—Did not Mr. Clark formerly reside in Queen Anne's District?

He did years ago.

9th Question.—How do you know that John Buckmaster is living in Washington City, and how do you know he has been there for eighteen months?

I saw him in Washington; he told me he was working at McDermot's Coach Factory. Mr. Gardner showed me on his books the morning he settled with him, the day he left on the cars.

10th Question.—How long has Mr. Wethers been conductor on the Baltimore and Potomac Railroad, and did he not have his family with him while in this county?

I do not know how long he was conductor, but I think it was over twelve months; he had his family with him at different places in the county.

11th Question.—Did or not colored voters occupy exclusively the door leading to the polls, until eleven or twelve o'clock on the day of election, in the Third Election District, and did not colored speakers, non-residents of the county, occupy the Court House yard while the voting was going on, haranguing and endeavoring thereby to excite and influence them from voting the Democratic ticket?

No, sir, they did not exclusively occupy the polls; there was a colored man speaking in the yard, a stranger to me; he was not interrupting any one; they did not undertake to excite or influence the colored voters.

B. F. DUVALL.

Test: RUFUS BELT.

DEPOSITION No. 22.

1st Question.—State your name, age, residence, occupation, and where you voted on the 4th day of November, 1873.

[Objected to by Mr. Brooke, on the ground that no such name appears upon the list of witnesses furnished by R. S. Widdicombe; Justice ruled that it was a misnomer, and evidence admitted.]

My name is Thomas H. Jackson; age, I cant' say exactly, but am over 57; I live in Marlboro' District; occupation, laborer; I voted in Marlboro District.

2d Question.—State how you voted, and if you voted the Democratic ticket.

I voted the Democratic ticket.

3d Question.—State if any efforts were made to induce you to vote the Democratic ticket; if yea, by whom, and what the efforts were.

Mr. Smallwood told me I would have to vote that ticket, or go to the penitentiary, one or the other; Mr. Wedding told me that I had better do it than be sent away; Mr. McCullough told me it was the best thing I could do; I would not be disturbed until Court was called; then I would be taken up and sent away. Of course, therefore, I did.

4th Question.—Was it not your desire and intention to vote the Republican ticket, and did you not vote against your sentiments in voting the Democratic ticket, and were you not induced to vote the Democratic ticket from fear?

It was my desire and intention to vote the Republican ticket; I voted against my sentiments; I was induced to vote from fear.

Cross-examined:

1st Question.—Can you read or write?

No, sir.

2d Question.—How can you tell a Republican ticket from a Democratic ticket?

Because I had seen them.

3d Question.—Who gave you the ticket that you voted?
Mr. McCullough.

4th Question.—Do you know if said ticket was marked or not?

I do not know.

5th Question.—Did you not state your intention to vote for Mr. Henry Brooke repeatedly, before the election?

No; I did not; I did at one time.

6th Question.—Do you know, of your own knowledge, that the name of Mr. Brooke was upon your ticket?

I do not.

7th Question.—Why were you induced by fear to vote that ticket?

They told me I had a piece of calico, but I did not know anything about it.

Re-cross-examined:

1st Question.—Was not the ticket voted by you the same given by Mr. George McCullough, after making the threat referred to in your examination-in-chief, and is not Mr. McCullough a Democrat, an active worker for Brooke on the day of election, and did he not tell you that Mr. Brooke's name was on the ticket?

It was the same ticket; I don't know, and did not know then, that Mr. McCullough was a Democrat; I really don't know that he was an active worker on the day of election; I don't recollect of his telling me that Mr. Brooke's name was on the ticket?

2d Question.—In asking you to vote, did not Mr. McCullough ask you to vote for Henry Brooke?

I don't recollect.

Re-cross-examined:

1st Question.—Did not Mr. McCullough come to you after the election, tell you he knew positively that you had not voted the ticket he gave you?

[Objection made by Mr. Brooke, counsel for Mr. Widdicombe, on the ground that it was not responsive to, nor had any connection with any matter brought out on the examination-in-chief, and a personal conversation which occurred after the election; objection overruled on the ground that it was pertinent to the examination-in-chief.]

He did, sir.

2d Question.—Have you told no one that you did not vote the ticket McCullough gave you?

I have not, sir.

THOMAS ⊢ JACKSON.
HIS
MARK.

Test: RUFUS BELT.

DEPOSITION No. 23.

1st Question.—State your name, age, residence, occupation, and where you voted on the 4th of November, 1873?

My name is Benedict Yost; in my 63d year; residence proper, Bladensburg; occupation, blacksmith; I voted in Bladensburg.

2d Question.—Were you or were you not a Judge of the Election, held on the 4th of November, 1873?

I was.

3d Question.—Do you or not know of any one voting in your district on said election day, whose names did not appear on the books of registration and the poll-book, and who were not legally qualified voters; was not the election fairly conducted and unusually quiet?

No, sir; I think so, sir; I know of nothing to the contrary.

Cross-examination:

1st Question.—What is your present occupation?

I am employed at present in the United States Custom House.

BENEDICT YOST.

Test: RUFUS BELT.

[Mr. Roberts, counsel for Mr. Brooke, the Contestant, after Benedict Yost had signed his deposition, but before he left the witness-stand, or the room in which said testimony was being taken, prayed the Justice to propound to him the following question:

"You have stated you were one of the Judges of Election on the 4th day of November, 1873; please state whether you were the Republican Judge, or one of the Democratic Judges?"

The Justice overruled the right of Mr. Brooke to re-call said witness for further cross-examination, upon the ground that he had signed his testimony, and his examination was concluded, to which ruling of the Justice the Contestant, by his counsel, excepted and prayed the Justice to note the same upon the testimony.

[Exceptions of Mr. Roberts, counsel for Mr. Brooke, filed ————, in the proceedings, upon the testimony of Benedict Yost.]

DEPOSITION No. 24.

1st Question.—State your name, age, residence, occupation, and where you voted on the 4th day of November, 1873.

My name is H. Eugene Brooke; age, 30 years; occupation, gentleman of elegant leisure; residence, Prince George's County, Md. ; I voted in the Second Election District, on the 4th of November, 1873.

2d Question.—How long have you voted in this county or district, and have you ever voted or offered to vote elsewhere?

I have voted in this county since the enfranchisement of parties who participated in the rebellion, and have voted in the district since 1869 ; before that time I voted in Nottingham; I have never voted, or offered, or desired to vote elsewhere.

3d Question.—How long have you resided in this county, and have you ever lost your residence in the county ?

I had the good fortune to be born here, and do not think I have ever lost my residence.

4th Question.—Do you know of any non-residents who voted the Democratic ticket, at your polls in Prince George's County, or elsewhere in Prince George's, at the election held on the 4th day of November, 1873 ; if yea, give name or names, and state all you know concerning the matter?

The question of residence is one I do not feel competent to determine, but if the Democratic interpretation be correct, that all parties who were staying out of the county are non-residents, I do know several. I know Aquilla H. Wilson, John T. Lowe, familiarly called Jack ; Daniel Clark, John Buckmaster, H. Brune Bowie, John F. Mudd, and Robert Bowie, of Walter ; I know that Wilson resides in Baltimore ; that he has been out of the county, both in Washington and Baltimore, for at least three years. I saw him in Marlboro' on the day of election. He reproached me for assisting in electing the Republican ticket, and stated that he had come to the poll and voted for the nominees of the Democratic party. I saw Mr. Lowe in Marlboro' upon the day of election. He stated to me that he voted, but did not say how ; I know that he resides in Baltimore City, and that he has been there for two or three years ; has his family there, and has invited me to his house. I know Mr. Clark has resided in Washington and Baltimore for several years, with his family, and I believe practiced law in each place. He was a nominee of the Democratic party, and I have every reason to believe, from his speeches, that he voted the Democratic ticket. I know John Buckmaster ; know that he resides in Washington, and had for one year prior to the election ; he told me that he was coming down particularly to vote for Henry Brooke and S. T. Suit, and afterward told me he had done so. I know H. Brune Bowie ; know that he is married, and living in Baltimore with his wife, and had been there at least one year prior to the 4th of November, 1873 ; he told me that he had come from Baltimore for the purpose of voting and supporting the Democratic ticket, and particularly Mr. Brooke, and had it not been for himself and two others in the Seventh District, the result would have been different. I was in Nottingham, at the polls, on 4th day of November, 1873, a part of the day ; saw both John F. Mudd and Robert Bowie, of Walter ; I had a conversation with Mudd there and previous, relative to his uncle, who was a candidate upon the Democratic ticket ; can't say that he voted the entire Democratic ticket, but from his conversation, am satisfied that he voted for the Contestant. Mr. Mudd resides in Baltimore with his wife and family, and has resided there at least two years prior to November 4th, 1873. Mr. Robert Bowie, of Walter, resides, I think, in Annapolis with his family, and has not, to my knowledge, ever resided in Nottingham District ; he voted an open ticket, and as I was standing by the side of him when he voted, I can assert that it was a Democratic ticket.

5th Question.—Do you know or not Albert Brooke, George Bowling, George W. Jackson, Samuel Williams and Minor Pose ; and have you ever had conversation with either or all of them about their residence ; or are you personally acquainted with the facts ; if yea, state fully all you know about it.

I am personally acquainted with all of the parties; I have had conversation with them all; they have always expressed their intention and desire to claim Prince George's, and Prince George's only, as their place of residence; and I believe them each and every one to be qualified voters of this county.

6th Question.—Did you or not tell Mr. W. B. Bowie or any one else that you had removed permanently from Prince George's County; and have you ever had a conversation with said Bowie on the subject; and, if so, state it?

I never told Mr. Bowie or any one else two years ago, or at any other time, that I had removed permanently; nor had I ever any such intention; I had conversations with Bowie upon the subject first in 1870, and declared to him my intention of voting here; shortly before the late election I met Mr. Bowie, and told him that I understood that my name had been taken from the books of registration; he informed me that my informant was a liar, that he had not taken it off, and had no such intention; I then notified him that I intended to claim this as my residence.

7th Question.—Do you know Thomas H. Hyde; do you know if he voted on the 4th day of November, 1873, and where and how did said Hyde vote?

I am acquainted with Hyde; he did vote at Marlboro'; Mr. Hyde came to me in Nottingham and asked me to bring him to Marlboro', stating that he desired to vote the entire Democratic ticket excepting S. T. Suit and B. F. Duvall; I declined to bring him; he was brought to Marlboro' by Jesse Ryon; on my way from Nottingham to Marlboro', I met Mr. Ryon returning, who informed me that that ticket that I scratched would not win; that he had made him put through a clean Democratic sheet; when I reached Marlboro' I saw Hyde; he told me it was no go, they would not let him vote for Suit; he had voted for all the Democrats.

8th Question.—Did you have a conversation with Jeremiah Coffren, officer of Registration for Nottingham District, about the legality of Ambrose and Hamilton Carroll's vote?

I did have a conversation with Coffren on the day of election, in Nottingham, relative to these two voters and some others, where slight clerical errors had occurred; after Mr. Coffren returned to the place of voting—having absented himself in the early part of the day—I mentioned the names of the two parties above to Mr Coffren ; he stated there had been a good deal of doubt about their right to vote, and many statements in regard to the same, but he reckoned they really had a right to vote ; and upon this statement I told them I thought they were safe in so doing.

9th Question.—State how long you have voted in Prince George's County, and if any objection was ever raised to your vote, so long as you were identified with the Democratic party?

I stated that before, in my examination. There never was any objection that I know of whilst I acted with the Democratic party ; on the contrary, they always seemed delighted to see me, or any parties I might bring with me, in securing the success of the Democratic ticket.

10th Question.—Was there or not ample opportunity and time between the opening and closing of the polls on the 4th day of November, 1873, for any person desiring to vote to do so ; and was not the election, in your opinion, fairly conducted ; and was or was not the election a fair expression of the legally qualified voters ; and do you know of any person or persons who voted, whose name does not apppear on the registration list?

I was at Nottingham District on the day of election until nearly three o'clock; there was ample time and opportunity for all voters to vote that desired to do so ; in fact, by the time I left, the voting was comparatively over ; I then came to Marlboro', found no difficulty in depositing my ballot, and, everything was going on quietly ; the election, in my opinion, was as fair as I have ever seen one ; and I really think the result was a fair expression of the legally qualified voters ; I saw no one vote except those whose names were on the registration list.

Cross-examination :

1st Question.—How long have you resided in Prince George's County ? Have you not resided with your family and been engaged in business in Washington City for nearly two years prior to the last election, or for what period of time, and how were you engaged ?

I claim to have a residence in Prince George's County since

the 16th day of March, 1844; that being the day of my birth; I have been in Washington temporarily engaged in business of different sorts for the purpose of making a living for my family—finding I could not do so under Democratic rule in Prince George's; my family have been in Washington during the winter and fall months, boarding there; summers have been spent elsewhere; my business connections in Washington ceased at least one year prior to the 4th of November, 1873.

2d Question.—Since you ceased doing business in Washington, where have you resided and for what time?

My time has been spent in various places for the purpose of settling up any business that I previously had, and in trying to procure employment for the purpose of maintaining myself and family in an honorable way.

3d Question.—You have stated your occupation, at present, was that of a gentleman of elegant leisure; now state if or not you have been engaged by Mr. Widdicombe as one of his clerks?

Mr. Widdicombe being unjustly deprived of his rights and employment, in my opinion, needs no clerk; I am not now employed, but presume that should he get his just rights, I can consider myself so engaged.

4th Question.—If the Democratic interpretation of residence, as stated by you, be correct, are you not a non-resident of this county?

If the construction put upon it by the Contestant in his case be correct, I should think that I, or any other person who left this county, matters not for what purpose or for what length of time, would have no residence in this county or elsewhere, unless I saw fit to vote a Democratic ticket.

5th Question.—Do you or not know if the residence of the parties referred to by you in your examination-in-chief, in Baltimore and Washington City, is permanent or temporary?

I cannot speak positively or knowingly of them all; but I have heard one of the parties, Mr. John F. Mudd, say that he never expected to come back here to live.

6th Question.—Does not John F. Mudd own and work a farm in this county?

Not that I know of.

7th Question.—Do you or not know that Robert Bowie, of Walter, is temporarily employed in the office of the State Treasurer ; that his wife owns a farm in this county, and that during the year 1873 he rented a house in this county in which he resided with his family in Nottingham District?

I do not know what office he is in, if temporary or permanent, I can't say. I think his wife owns some land in the county, in Nottingham District. I have no knowledge that he rented a house or resided in Nottingham District.

8th Question.—Has not Daniel Clark a law office in Marlboro', and does he not practice law here ?

Mr. Clark has his sign upon an office in Marlboro'; I seldom or ever see it open, nor do I know the contents of it ; I know that Mr. Clark practices law in Marlboro'.

9th Question.—Do you or not know if, after Mr. Clark resided in Washington, as you have stated, he returned to this county and resided here with his family for some time prior to going to Baltimore?

He may have done so ; but if so, it certainly was more than twelve months prior to the election.

10th Question.—Has your family ever resided in the Third Election District of said county, and if so, for what period of time ; and during said residence, if any, were they housekeeping, boarding or visiting ?

If my mother's farm or a portion of it is in the Third District, which I think it is, then I lived in said district about eighteen months from about November, 1868, until 1870 ; during which time I boarded with my mother.

11th Question.—In what election district was your farm situated, and did you dispose of the same and all of your property in this county before you went to Washington, or soon after ?

My farm was in Nottingham District, immediately on the line between Marlboro' and Nottingham ; I disposed of the farm, but not of all the property I owned in the county, nor had not disposed of the same prior to the election.

12th Question.—What property did you own in this county within twelve months prior to said election?

Several articles of personal property at my brother's, consisting of a horse and other personal property of that kind, and indebtedness due me by citizens of the county.

11

13th Question.—Since you engaged in business in Washington, have you ever brought your family to this county, except upon a visit, prior to the election?

I have not.

14th Question.—In your examination-in-chief you have stated you believed Albert Brooke, George Bowling, George W. Jackson, Samuel Williams and Minor Pose, residents and qualified voters in this county, and further stated that Daniel Clarke, John T. Low, Aquilla Wilson, John Buckmaster, J. F. Mudd and Robert Bowie, of W. & H. Brune Bowie, did not reside in the county; do you or not think the last named parties are entitled to a vote and residence in this county, equally with the parties first named? And, if not, your reason?

I think so far as the residence of a majority are concerned they are about equally entitled to vote; I have heard the first named declare their intentions to retain their residence here; never had heard the last named parties, excepting Mr. Clark, and that during his speeches in the campaign; George Bowling I do not consider a similar case to the parties named, being quite largely interested in real estate in this county and spending much of his time here improving the same.

15th Question.—Does not George Bowling own real estate in Washington City, and has he not resided there for the past two years and more prior to the election, and has he not been improving the same?

I have understood that he owned property there; he has resided there, but for what length of time I can't say; I do not know that he has been improving the same.

16th Question.—On what street, Legislative District and number of the house of Washington City was your family living on the 16th of September, 1872 and 1873?

To the best of my knowledge and belief, I do not think they were residing there either of the time.

17th Question.—Have you voted in this county every election since you were enfranchised? And, if not, state at what election you did not vote.

I have voted at every election in Prince George's County since my enfranchisement except one, when I was detained in St. Mary's County, Md., by unavoidable circumstances; that was in the year 1872.

18th Question.—You have stated you saw no one vote except those whose names were upon the registration books? Did you or not see the names of all who did vote upon those books?

I did not, it being in the hand of the Judges of Election; I heard no complaint of such an offence.

19th Question.—Did you ever reside in the Sixteenth Legislative District of Washington City?

Never prior to the election.

H. EUGENE BROOKE.

Test: RUFUS BELT.

DEPOSITION NO. 25.

1st Question.—State your name, age, residence, occupation, and where you voted on the 4th day of November, 1873.

My name is John E. Gardner; age, 43 years; residence, Upper Marlboro'; occupation, one-horse tavern-keeper; voted in Marlboro' District.

2d Question.—Do you know Thomas Hyde; if he voted on the 4th of November, 1873; where he voted and how he voted, and if said Hyde was an unpardoned convict?

I know Hyde; he voted in Marlboro' District on the 4th of November, 1873; do not know how he voted; do not know that he is an unpardoned convict.

3d Question.—Do you know John Buckmaster; where he voted on the 4th of November, 1873; how he voted, and if he is a non-resident of Prince George's County?

I know Buckmaster; he voted in Marlboro' District on the 4th of November, 1873. He asked witness if there was any one he wished him to vote for; that he was going to vote the Democratic ticket. Witness told him there was; he then handed witness his Democratic ticket, and witness crossed the name of Daniel Clark, and inserted that of S. T. Suit in its place; there was no other name erased from the ticket. Subsequently Buckmaster told witness he had voted the ticket he wished. He has not been living in the county more than a year; think he left some time in 1872; he says he lives in Washington.

4th Question.—Were you present during the day, on the 4th of November, 1873, at the voting place in said Third Election District? If so, state if, in your opinion, said election was not fairly conducted.

I was present part of the time, but I saw no disturbance.

Cross-examined :

1st Question.—Do you or not know if the removal of John Buckmaster to Washington is temporary or permanent, and if he ever voted there?

I can't say ; never saw him from the time he left, until the night before the election ; do not know that he ever voted there.

JOHN E. GARDNER.

Test : RUFUS BELT.

DEPOSITION No. 26.

1st Question.—State your name, age, residence, occupation, and where you voted on the 4th of November, 1873.

My name is Edward Jones ; age, 38 years ; residence, Upper Marlboro', Md.; occupation, printer ; voted in the Third Election District.

2d Question.—Do you know Aquilla Wilson and John F. Lowe? If so, state where they reside, where they voted on the 4th of November, 1873, and how they voted.

I know them ; both live in Baltimore with their families ; they have been living there three or four years. I did not see the votes put in the ballot-box. Both told me they voted the Democratic ticket, in the Third Election District, Prince George's County. Mr. Lowe remarked that he had a good thing of it, if the Democratic party carried the county.

Cross-examination :

1st Question.—Do you or not know if the removal of said parties to Baltimore was temporary or permanent, and if they have not always claimed their residence and voted here since?

I do not know if it be temporary or permanent; I do not know that they claimed their residence here, but know they have voted here since, but not how often.

ED. JONES.

Test : RUFUS BELT.

DEPOSITION No. 27.

1st Question.—State your name, age, occupation, residence and where you voted on the 4th day of November, 1873?

My name is John W. Duvall ; age, 37 years ; occupation, farmer ; residence, Prince George's County ; I voted in Upper Marlboro'.

2d Question.—State if you know Aquilla Wilson, John T. Lowe, generally called Jack Lowe, and where they reside; state also, if you know George Bowling, and if you have had any conversation with him in reference to his voting, and his desire and intention of continuing the same?

As for Mr. Wilson, he has been away from the county for some years, living in Baltimore, I believe. Jack Lowe has been working in the tobacco warehouse for two or three years. George Bowling, about twelve or eighteen months ago, told me that he did not think he would ever come back here to live, but he always intended to hold property here, so that he could continue the right to vote here.

3d Question.—State if you were present on the 4th of day November, 1873, and about the polls, and if you consider said election fairly conducted?

I was around about the polls all day, excepting about half an hour at dinner; I never saw a fairer election.

JOHN W. DUVALL.

Test : RUFUS BELT.

DEPOSITION No. 28.

1st Question.—State your name, age, residence, occupation, and where you voted on the 4th of November, 1873?

My name is Lemuel Porter; am over 52 years of age; residence, Huntington City; occupation, merchant; did not vote.

2d Question.—State, if you please, if you know John G. Seitz, and if you know how long he has resided in the State of Maryland, and when he came to said State?

I know him; he came to Maryland between the 12th and 20th of November, 1872.

3d Question.—State where he was residing prior to that time?

He was residing at Watsontown, Northumberland County, Pa.; the reason I know, I held the vendue, and sold his goods in my name, at his house, the 9th of November, 1872, in Pennsylvania; he was residing there at that time; he was at the sale.

Cross-examined :

1st Question.—Did not Seitz reside in some part of Maryland some time previous to November, 1872?

He told me he had lived in Maryland at one time, but he had lived in Watsontown eighteen months previous to the 9th of November, 1872, and that he had lived in other parts of Pennsylvania, prior to his coming to Watsontown.

LEMUEL PORTER.

Test : Rufus Belt.

Deposition No. 29.

1st Question.—State your name, age, residence, occupation, and where you voted on the 4th day of November, 1873?

My name is Daniel A. Jenkins ; age, 37 years ; residence, Prince George's County ; occupation, agent ; voted in Queen Anne District.

2d Question.—State, if you please, if you know John G. Seitz ; if he voted on the 4th of November, 1873 ; if yea, state where he voted, if he voted the Democratic or Republican ticket, and state all you know about it ?

I do not know, of my own knowledge, that he voted at all. I heard him say that he voted for Henry Brooke ; he did not say where he voted. I know that he claims his residence in Vansville District, Prince George's County, and was registered there ; he said he voted for Mr. Brooke at the last election, held on the 4th of November, 1873.

3d Question.—Do you know J. Lack Higgins, where he resides, where he voted on the 4th of November, 1873, and if he voted the Democratic or Republican ticket ?

I know him ; his family resides in Anne Arundel County ; he is employed on the Baltimore and Philadelphia Railroad ; he told me he voted at Marlboro', and asked me if the Bowie House was in Marlboro' District ; the Bowie House is where he boards ; he told me he voted for Henry Brooke ; the Bowie House is in Vansville District.

Cross-examined :

1st Question.—Where do you reside and board, and did you vote at the late election, and where ?

Reside in Prince George's County ; board with Mr. Jacobs ; voted in Queen Anne.

2d Question.—How long have you been a resident of this county ?

Since November 1st, 1872.

3d Question.—Where did you reside prior to November 1st, 1872?

Baltimore.

4th Question.—Did you not vote, in the fall of 1872, at an election in Baltimore?

I did.

5th Question.—At what election in 1872 did you vote?

I voted at the municipal election.

6th Question.—Did you not vote at the Presidential election in 1872?

No, sir.

DANIEL A. JENKINS.

Test: RUFUS BELT.

DEPOSITION NO. 30.

1st Question.—State your name, age, residence, occupation, and where you voted on the 4th of November, 1873.

My name is George C. Merrick ; age, 34 years ; residence, Prince George's County ; occupation, attorney-at-law ; voted in the Third Election District (Marlboro').

2d Question.—State if you know the following parties : Aquilla Wilson, John T. Lowe, familiarly known as Jack Lowe, Daniel Clark, John Buckmaster, Michael Sparrow, H. Bruno Bowie, John F. Mudd, and Walter W. W. Bowie ; and if you do, where do they reside ; and if they voted in Prince George's County on the 4th of November, 1873 ; how they voted, and all you know about their voting.

I know all of the above-named parties ; Aquilla Wilson lives in Baltimore ; has lived there for several years ; do not know where he voted or how he voted. Lowe has been living in Baltimore for several years ; do not know where he voted or how he voted, but know that they claimed to be Democrats. Daniel Clark has been living with his family in Baltimore for several years ; do not think he owns any property in the county ; he voted at Upper Marlboro' on the 4th of November, 1873 ; do not know how he voted, but suppose he voted the Democratic ticket, as he was the Democratic candidate for the State Senate. I do not know where Buckmaster resides, or if he voted at all. Michael Sparrow resides in Baltimore City ; has been residing there for several years ; engaged in one calling or another, so he has told me ; he also told me that he had not been to Prince George's County, to attend the elections regularly, but that he felt a great interest in the last election, both on account of friends, and his desire to see the Republican ticket defeated ; he came to Prince George's County, and voted the Democratic ticket in Queen Anne ; do not believe that he owns any property in Prince George's County. H. Brune Bowie married in Baltimore, and is now living there, where he has been living for two years or more ; I heard him say to Captain Widdicombe that he was a clever fellow, and he regretted that he had been compelled to work against him and vote against him at the last election ; do not think he owns any property in the county. John F. Mudd resides in Baltimore, and is in business with Dyon Hill & Co.; has resided there for several years. I think Walter W. W. Bowie is living in Baltimore with his family, and has re-sided there for several years ; engaged in the practice of law, and also, I think, assistant editor of the *American Farmer ;* I do not know how he voted, or if he voted at all. I do not know how Mudd voted, or if he voted at all.

Cross-examined :

1st Question.—Has not Daniel Clark a law office in Upper Marlboro', and has he not been engaged in practicing law here for a number of years ?

He has an office in Marlboro', and has been engaged in the practice of law at this bar since I first knew him, but since his removal from the county, his visits to Marlboro' and his office have been transient, such as any other lawyer living in the city would be compelled to make, to attend to any case he might have in the county.

2d Question.—Does he not generally attend each term of our Court, through the entire session, and often between terms ?

He does generally attend the terms of our Court, and re-mains as long as the urgency of his business requires him, which frequently detains him during the entire term ; he visits the county seat also, between the terms, whenever his busi-brings him here.

3d Question.—Do you not know Jack Lowe, A. Wilson, John Buckmaster, Michael S. Sparrow, A. Brune Bowie, John F. Mudd, W. W. W. Bowie and Daniel Clark ? Have all not for years claimed their residence in Prince George's County and have been voting here?

Jack Lowe and Wilson, I believe, have been voting in Prince George's County for some years; I have no means of knowing where they claim their residence except from the fact they have voted here, and infer from that that they claim their residence here; of Buckmaster I know but little; some two years ago, I think, he lived and voted here; since then I have lost sight of him; I do not know, except from what Mr. Sparrow told me, where he has been voting; said he claimed Prince George's as his residence, but had not attended the elections regularly; H. Brune Bowie and W. W. W. Bowie, Daniel Clark and John F. Mudd have claimed this county, I know, as their residence, and I believe have been voting here.

GEORGE C. MERRICK.

Test: RUFUS BELT.

DEPOSITION No. 31.

1st Question.—State your name, age, residence, occupation, and where you voted on the 4th day of November, 1873.

Name, R. H. Beall; age, 55 years; residence, Nottingham District; occupation, farmer; I voted in Nottingham District.

2d Question.—State how long you have resided in Prince George's County, below Upper Marlboro', and whether or not the visit of Dr. John H. Skinner to New Orleans, on business connected with the Fowler estate, was subsequent or prior to your residence in Prince George's County below Upper Marlboro'?

I have resided more than twenty-one years below Upper Marlboro'; Dr. Skinner went South before I went to live below Marlboro'.

3d Question—Has Dr. Skinner been South since your residence in that portion of the county?

I do not think he has; I never heard that he had; I am pretty sure he has not.

4th Question.—Do you know John F. Mudd? If yea, state where he resides, how long he has been residing there, and where he voted on the 4th of November, 1873?

I know Mudd; he resides in Baltimore City; I think he has been there four years, I know, and I think longer; he voted at Nottingham on the 4th of November, 1873, in Prince George's County.

5th Question.—Do you know Ambrose Carroll and Hamilton Carroll; if or not any threats or intimidation were used to prevent their voting at the last election; and, if so, what were the threats, where made and by whom?

[Question No. 5 withdrawn.]

I know them both; Mr. Coffren, the Register, came up by my house, riding up in the yard, talking about the house.

Cross-examined:

1st Question.—You have stated that John F. Mudd resides in Baltimore City and has been there for four years; now state if Mr. Mudd does not own and work a farm in Prince George's County?

If he does I do not know of it.

2d Question.—Do you or not know if or not Mr. Mudd voted in this county prior to the 4th of November, 1873? If yea, state where and when?

He used to vote there when he lived at his mother's place, prior to November, 1873; do not know how long he voted there prior to November last.

3d Question.—Do you or not know that Mr. Mudd, since he has been doing business in Baltimore, has returned to this county to vote at any of the elections held prior to the 4th of November, 1873?

I am not able to answer the question.

R. H. BEALL.

Test: RUFUS BELT.

EXHIBITS.

EXHIBIT No. 1.

STATE OF MARYLAND, PRINCE GEORGE'S COUNTY, SCT:

On this fourth day of November, 1873, personally appeared James Harris, and John W. Medley, and T. E. Williams, before the subscriber, one of the Judges of Election of the Third Election District of said County, and duly qualified as Clerks of Elections in the Third Election District of the County aforesaid, according to the Acts of Assembly in such cases made and provided.

RECTOR PUMPHREY.

STATE OF MARYLAND, PRINCE GEORGE'S COUNTY, SCT:

I HEREBY CERTIFY, That the above is a true extract taken from the Poll Books of the Third Election District for Prince George's County, Maryland, now on file in my office.

In testimony whereof, I hereunto subscribe my name and affix the seal of the Circuit Court for Prince [SEAL.] George's County, this 22d day of January, Anno Domini, 1874.

HENRY BROOKE,

Clerk of the Circuit Court for Prince George's County, Md.

Filed with me this 26th day of January, 1874.

[SEAL.] JAMES HARRIS,

Justice of the Peace.

EXHIBIT No. 2.

CIRCUIT COURT FOR PRINCE GEORGE'S COUNTY, ⎱
APRIL TERM, 1853. ⎰

STATE OF MARYLAND

vs.

THOMAS CONTEE WORTHINGTON.

1853, April 12th, Presentment and Indictment for the murder of Charles Crook; appears and arraigned. Suggestion and affidavit filed; order for removal of case to Anne Arundel County filed.

CIRCUIT COURT FOR PRINCE GEORGE'S COUNTY, ⎱
APRIL TERM, 1853. ⎰

We, the Grand Inquest of the State of Maryland for the body of Prince George's County, do, on our oaths, present Dr. Thos. C. Worthington, on the testimony of Dr. Jno. M. S. Maccubbin, Dr. Thomas G. Turton, Robert Thompson, Wm. N. Burch, W. H. Grimes, Robert W. G. Baden, Dr. John H. Skinner, M. J. Kaldenbach, John A. Goldsborough and Thomas A. T. Ball, for the murder of Charles Crook, on the 22d day of November, in the year eighteen hundred and fifty-two.

HENRY JONES, *Foreman.*

STATE OF MARYLAND, PRINCE GEORGE'S COUNTY, SCT:

I HEREBY CERTIFY, That the aforegoing is truly taken and copied from the Minutes and Proceedings of the Circuit Court for Prince George's County at the April Term, 1853, thereof.

In testimony whereof, I hereunto subscribe my name and affix the seal of the Circuit Court for Prince George,s County, this twenty-second day of January, Anno Domini, 1874.

[SEAL.]

HENRY BROOKE,
Clerk of the Circuit Court for Prince George's County, Md.

Filed with me this 26th day of January, 1874.

[SEAL.]

JAMES HARRIS,
Justice of the Peace.

EXHIBIT No. 3.

ELECTION DISTRICTS	Candidate	No. 1	No. 2	No. 3	No. 4	No. 5	No. 6	No. 7	No. 8	No. 9	No. 10	No. 11	Total
For Comptroller of Treasury.	Levin Woolford	275	293	228	158	269	229	207	195	95	193	118	2,263
	Henry H. Goldsborough	188	319	428	219	307	268	267	156	103	131	143	2,429
For Clerk of Court of Appeals.	James S. Franklin	274	295	328	158	269	221	207	125	91	173	118	2,262
	John H. Price	188	317	498	219	307	268	268	156	104	131	143	2,429
For Senate of Md...	Daniel Clarke	309	305	322	157	273	195	215	126	91	180	119	2,292
	Samuel T. Suit	140	294	431	218	292	292	260	155	108	123	143	2,366
For House of Delegates	George W. Wilson	294	294	338	156	269	211	206	125	94	175	117	2,279
	Benjamin F. Grey	307	334	328	158	269	216	207	126	93	174	119	2,331
	Charles H. Stanley	289	290	327	158	268	219	207	126	95	190	119	2,285
	Latimer A. Edelison	168	302	496	218	268	268	268	154	103	143	143	2,391
	Aaron V. B. Robey	163	287	419	220	267	267	268	155	103	143	143	2,348
	William Latchford	149	308	420	220	206	275	268	154	103	125	144	2,372
For Sheriff..........	John H. Underwood	276	324	324	157	286	211	208	113	101	176	109	2,182
	Harrison Wallis	188	386	432	230	184	278	265	170	98	129	143	2,493
For Clerk of Circuit Court.	Henry Brooke	288	279	361	160	275	233	211	131	94	182	128	2,342
	Robert S. Widdicombe	172	330	395	215	201	256	264	154	105	133	134	2,349
For County Commiss'rs	William B. Hill	290	291	327	158	265	214	206	120	94	172	118	2,255
	Joshua T. Clarke	303	294	325	157	269	213	214	127	96	176	116	2,290
	John V. Piles	272	289	303	165	270	231	202	120	96	173	118	2,241
	Benjamin F. Turton	271	280	327	157	298	213	201	118	96	123	115	2,226
	Lewis W. Jenkins	299	283	328	156	269	211	204	121	92	181	140	2,262
	Alexander P. Hill	168	316	430	220	269	278	268	163	104	127	140	2,420
	Fielder C. Duvall	197	349	429	220	206	274	278	160	101	125	143	2,486
	Benjamin Brashears	188	318	497	220	206	262	267	156	96	136	141	2,417
	Benjamin F. Duvall	165	310	455	221	206	271	260	163	96	128	140	2,497
	Thomas H. Lusby	153	312	426	290	208	271	262	160	102	136	147	2,387
For County Surveyor.	Robert A. Bowie	288	267	329	153	270	211	210	130	94	175	132	2,259
	George W. Jackson	174	341	427	220	206	277	264	153	105	129	139	2,425

To HENRY BROOKE, ESQ.,

Clerk of the Circuit Court for Prince George's County:

WHEREAS, an election for Comptroller of the Treasury of Maryland, Clerk of the Court of Appeals, a representative in the Senate of Maryland from Prince George's County, three representatives from said county in the House of Delegates, Clerk of the Circuit Court for Prince George's County, Sheriff, County Commissioners, and a County Surveyor, was held on the first Tuesday after the first Monday in November (being the fourth day of the month), in the year eighteen hundred and seventy-three, in the election districts in said county, distinguished by number one, etc., conformably to the constitution and laws of this State; and *whereas*, we, the subscribers, attending judges at the close of the election in said districts, having this day assembled at the usual place of the sitting of the Circuit Court for said county, with the books of the polls, on which are endorsed the several certificates agreeably to law, and having cast up the whole number of votes given in said districts, according to the certificates made out on the day of election by the judges, it appears that Henry H. Goldsborough has twenty-four hundred and twenty-nine votes for Comptroller of the Treasury; Levin Woolford, twenty-two hundred and sixty-three votes for Comptroller of the Treasury; that James S. Franklin has twenty-two hundred and sixty-two votes, and that John H. Price has twenty-four hundred and twenty-nine votes for Clerk of the Court of Appeals; that Samuel T. Suit has the greatest number of legal votes for the Senate of Maryland; that Latimer A. Etchison, Aaron V. B. Robey and William Latchford have the greatest number of legal votes for the House of Delegates; that Robert S. Widdicombe has the greatest number of legal votes for Clerk of the Circuit Court; that Harrison Wallis has the greatest number of legal votes for Sheriff; that Alexander P. Hill, Fielder C. Duvall, Benjamin Brashears, Benjamin F. Duvall and Thomas H. Lusby have the greatest number of legal votes for County Commissioners, and that George W. Jackson has the greatest number of legal votes for County Surveyor; whereupon, we do determine, declare and return that the said Samuel T. Suit, for Senate; Latimer A. Etchison, Aaron V.

Robey and William Latchford, for the House of Delegates; Robert S. Widdicombe, for Clerk of the Circuit Court; Harrison Wallis, for Sheriff; Alexander P. Hill, Fielder C. Duvall, Benjamin Brashears, Benjamin F. Duvall and Thomas H. Lusby, for County Commissioners, and George W. Jackson, for County Surveyor, are duly elected.

Given under our hands this sixth day of November, in the year eighteen hundred and seventy-three.

MARK DUVALL,	[SEAL.]
M. L. WILSON,	[SEAL.]
CHARLES BOWIE,	[SEAL.]
J. E. Q. EARLY,	[SEAL.]
GEORGE W. GARDINER,	[SEAL.]
JOSEPH SOPER,	[SEAL.]
JAMES MULLIKIN,	[SEAL.]
JAMES H. RAWLINGS,	[SEAL.]
W. PARKER GRIFFIN,	[SEAL.]
JOHN W. WHITESIDE,	[SEAL.]
WM. B. TOWNSHEND.	[SEAL.]

STATE OF MARYLAND, PRINCE GEORGE'S COUNTY, SCT:

I HEREBY CERTIFY, That the aforegoing and within is a true copy of the original election returns filed in the office of the Clerk of the Circuit Court for Prince George's County, on the sixth day of November, 1873.

In testimony whereof, I hereunto subscribe my name and affix the seal of the Circuit Court for Prince [SEAL.] George's County, this twenty-second day of January, Anno Domini, 1874.

HENRY BROOKE,

Clerk of the Circuit Court for Prince George's County, Md.

Filed with me this 26th day of January, 1874.

[SEAL.] JAMES HARRIS,

Justice of the Peace.

EXHIBIT No. 4.

State of Maryland, Prince George's County, Sct:

I hereby certify, That it appears by the Poll and Registration Books of the Seventh Election District of Prince George's County, Maryland, that Oden Williams and Charles Stewart were registered and voted in said District at the election held on the fourth day of November, 1873.

    In testimony whereof, I hereunto subscribe my name and affix the seal of the Circuit Court for Prince [SEAL.]   George's County, this twenty-second day of January, Anno Domini, 1874.

HENRY BROOKE,

Clerk of the Circuit Court for Prince George's County, Md.

Filed with me this 26th day of January, 1874.

[SEAL.]   JAMES HARRIS,

Justice of the Peace.

EXHIBIT No. 5.

State of Maryland, Prince George's County, Sct:

I hereby certify, That it appears, by the Poll Books of the Ninth Election District of Prince George's County, Maryland, that James Young voted in said District, at the election held on the fourth day of November, 1873.

    In testimony whereof, I hereunto subscribe my name and affix the seal of the Circuit Court for Prince [SEAL.]   George's County, this twenty-second day of January, Anno Domini, 1874.

HENRY BROOKE,

Clerk of the Circuit Court for Prince George's County, Md.

Filed with me this 26th day of January, 1874.

[SEAL.]   JAMES HARRIS,

Justice of the Peace.

EXHIBIT No. 6.

STATE OF MARYLAND, PRINCE GEORGE'S COUNTY, SCT:

I HEREBY CERTIFY, That it appears by the Poll Books of the Third Election District of Prince George's County, Maryland, that James Young voted in said District at the election held on the fourth day of November, 1873.

In testimony whereof, I hereunto subscribe my name and affix the seal of the Circuit Court for Prince [SEAL.] George's County, this 22d day of January, Anno Domini, 1874.

HENRY BROOKE,

Clerk of the Circuit Court for Prince George's County, Md.

Filed with me this 26th day of January, 1874.
[SEAL.]   JAMES HARRIS,
                         Justice of the Peace.

———.

EXHIBIT No. 7.

STATE OF MARYLAND, PRINCE GEORGE'S COUNTY, MD.

I HEREBY CERTIFY, That it appears from the Registration Book of the Third Election District of Prince George's County, Maryland, that James Young was registered as a qualified voter in said district upon a certificate of transfer from the Sixth (Spalding's) Election District of said county.

In testimony whereof, I hereunto subscribe my name and affix the seal of the Circuit Court for Prince [SEAL.] George's County, this 22d day of January, Anno Domini, 1874.

HENRY BROOKE,

Clerk of the Circuit Court for Prince George's County, Md.

Filed with me this 26th day of January, 1874.
[SEAL.]   JAMES HARRIS,
                         Justice of the Peace.

12

EXHIBIT No. 8.

State of Maryland, Prince George's County, Sct:

I hereby certify, That the names of Charles H. Walker, Patrick Ferquher and Charles H. Dickinson appear upon the Registration Books of the Second Election District of Prince George's County, Maryland, but that in the column of qualified voters a mark of the pen has been made through each of said names; but no entry of the cause or reason of disqualification of either of said parties appear upon said book.

In testimony whereof, I hereunto subscribe my name and affix the seal of the Circuit Court for Prince [SEAL.]   George's County, this 22d day of January, Anno Domini, 1874.

HENRY BROOKE,

Clerk of the Circuit Court for Prince George's County, Md.

Filed with me this 26th day of January, 1874.

[SEAL.]   ·   JAMES HARRIS,

Justice of the Peace.

EXHIBIT No. 9.

State of Maryland, Prince George's County, Sct:

I hereby certify, That the name of John N. Hayes appears upon the Registration Book of the Second Election District of Prince George's County, Maryland, as a qualified voter therein.

In testimony whereof, I hereunto subscribe my name and affix the seal of the Circuit Court for Prince [SEAL.]   George's County, this 22d day of January, Anno Domini, 1874.

HENRY BROOKE,

Clerk of the Circuit Court for Prince George's County, Md.

Filed with me this 26th day of January, 1874.

[SEAL.]   JAMES HARRIS,

Justice of the Peace.

EXHIBIT No. 10.

STATE OF MARYLAND, PRINCE GEORGE'S COUNTY, SCT:

I HEREBY CERTIFY, That the name of Jacob Oakey appears upon the Registration Book of the Seventh Election District of Prince George's County, Maryland, as a qualified voter.

       In testimony whereof, I hereunto subscribe my name
       and affix the seal of the Circuit Court for Prince
[SEAL.]   George's County, this 22d day of January, Anno
       Domini, 1874.

HENRY BROOKE,
Clerk of the Circuit Court for Prince George's County, Md.

Filed with me this 26th day of January, 1874.
[SEAL.]   JAMES HARRIS,
                      Justice of the Peace.

EXHIBIT No. 11.

STATE OF MARYLAND, PRINCE GEORGE'S COUNTY, SCT:

I HEREBY CERTIFY, That it appears, by the Poll Books of the Third Election District of Prince George's County, Maryland, that William Henry Holland voted in said district at the election held on the 4th day of November, 1873.

       In testimony whereof, I hereunto subscribe my name
       and affix the seal of the Circuit Court for Prince
[SEAL.]   George's County, this twenty-second day of Jan-
       uary, Anno Domini, 1874.

HENRY BROOKE,
Clerk of the Circuit Court for Prince George's County, Md.

Filed with me this 26th day of January, 1874.
[SEAL.]   JAMES HARRIS,
                      Justice of the Peace.

EXHIBIT No. 12.

STATE OF MARYLAND, PRINCE GEORGE'S COUNTY, SCT:

I HEREBY CERTIFY, That it appears, by the Poll Books of the Fourth Election District of Prince George's County, Maryland, that Ambrose Carroll and Wm. Hamilton Carroll voted in said district, at the election held on the 4th day of November, 1873.

   In testimony whereof, I hereunto subscribe my name
    and affix the seal of the Circuit Court for Prince
[SEAL.] George's County, Maryland, this twenty-second
    day of January, Anno Domini, 1874.
         HENRY BROOKE,
Clerk of the Circuit Court for Prince George's County, Md.

Filed with me this 26th day of January, 1874.
[SEAL.]   JAMES HARRIS,
         Justice of the Peace.

EXHIBIT No. 13.

CIRCUIT COURT FOR PRINCE GEORGE'S COUNTY, }
         APRIL TERM, 1870. }

STATE OF MARYLAND *vs.* MACK JOHNSON.	1870, April 9th, Presentment for Larceny. April 11th, Indictment filed. 1870, April 26th, prisoner arraigned, pleads Guilty and sentenced to the County Jail for thirty (30) days.

    Test: HENRY BROOKE, *Clerk, &c.*

STATE OF MARYLAND, PRINCE GEORGE'S COUNTY, SCT .

I HEREBY CERTIFY, That the aforegoing is truly taken and copied from the Minutes and Proceedings of the Circuit Court for Prince George's County.

   In testimony whereof, I have hereunto subscribed my
    name and affixed the seal of the Circuit Court for
[SEAL.] Prince George's County, this 16th day of January,
    Anno Domini, 1874.
         HENRY BROOKE,
Clerk of the Circuit Court for Prince George's County, Md.

Filed with me this 26th day of January, 1874.
[SEAL.]   JAMES HARRIS,
         Justice of the Peace..

EXHIBIT No. 14.

CIRCUIT COURT FOR PRINCE GEORGE'S COUNTY, }
NOVEMBER TERM, 1859. }

STATE OF MARYLAND

vs.

NACE BEALL.

} 1859, November 14th, Presentment and Indictment for Larceny.
Arraigned, pleads Not Guilty ; tried
by jury ; verdict, Guilty. Motion
for a new trial. 1859, November
15th, Motion withdrawn, and Court
sentenced him to be sold for five
years within the State of Maryland.

Test: HENRY BROOKE, *Clerk, &c.*

STATE OF MARYLAND, PRINCE GEORGE'S COUNTY, SCT:

HEREBY CERTIFY, That the aforegoing is truly taken and
copied from the Minutes and Proceedings of the Circuit Court
for Prince George's County.

In testimony whereof, I have hereunto subscribed my
name and affixed the seal of the Circuit Court for
[SEAL.]   Prince George's County, this 16th day of January,
Anno Domini, 1874.

HENRY BROOKE,
Clerk of the Circuit Court for Prince George's County, Md.

Filed with me this 26th day of January, 1874.
[SEAL.]   JAMES HARRIS,
Justice of the Peace.

EXHIBIT No. 15.

CIRCUIT COURT FOR PRINCE GEORGE'S COUNTY, }
APRIL TERM, 1868. }

STATE OF MARYLAND

vs.

GEORGE LOCKER.

} 1868, April 14, presentment for larceny.
1868, April 17, indictment filed.
1868, April 20, prisoner arraigned and
pleads Not Guilty. Jury sworn ; verdict, Guilty. 1868, April 28, sentenced
to the Penitentiary for one (1) year.

Test : HENRY BROOKE, *Clerk.*

State of Maryland, Prince George's County, Sct. :

I HEREBY CERTIFY, That the foregoing is truly taken and copied from the Minutes and Proceedings of the Circuit Court for Prince George's County.

      In testimony whereof, I have hereunto subscribed my [SEAL.] name and affixed the seal of the Circuit Court for Prince George's County, this 16th day of January, A. D., 1874.

HENRY BROOKE,

Clerk of the Circuit Court for Prince George's County, Md.

Filed with me this 26th day of January, 1874.

[SEAL.]   JAMES HARRIS,

Justice of the Peace.

R. S. W., No. 1..

In the case of Henry Brooke, contesting the election of R. S. Widdicombe, to the office of Clerk of the Circuit Court for Prince George's County :

    R. S. Widdicombe, by George C. Merrick, his attorney, objects to the evidence taken in the above case, under the two several notices in this case served on said Widdicombe, and signed and sealed by James Harris, Justice of the Peace, one dated 9th day of December, 1873, and the other dated 24th January, 1873, for the following reasons :

First. Because said notices state that the Justice of the Peace would begin to take testimony under said notices on days therein named, and continue from day to day until the same was completed, when, in point of fact, the taking of testimony has been suspended for several days together and then proceeded with, without any new or additional notices to said R. S. Widdicombe.

Secondly. Because said notices do not contain statements of the facts to be proved by the party applying for said notices, when the law expressly requires they should.

GEORGE C. MERRICK,

Attorney for R. S. Widdicombe.

Filed with me this 26th day of January, 1874.

[SEAL.]   JAMES HARRIS,

Justice of the Peace.

HENRY BROOKE.

_vs._

ROBERT S. WIDDICOMBE.

In the matter of the contest for the office of Clerk of the Circuit Court, for Prince George's County, Md. In the House of Delegates of Maryland.

Henry Brooke, the Contestant in the case, respectfully suggests to the Honorable the House of Delegates of Maryland, that the objections of R. S. Widdicombe to the evidence taken in said case, before James Harris, Justice of the Peace, should not be entertained, but the same should be dismissed by your Honorable body, for the following reasons :

First. Because said notices, under which that evidence was taken, expressly recite that the same " will be continued from day to day until the same is completed," and the same was done in strict conformity thereto ; that the intermissions in the taking of said proof were unavoidable and necessary to secure the attendance of the witnesses; that he examined no witness without first giving full notice to the said R. S. Widdicombe of his intention to do so, and that the said Widdicombe always, and in every instance, attended the examination of said witnesses, and cross-examined the same, and further that the examination of said witnesses was frequently and invariably postponed to suit the convenience of the said Widdicombe and his counsel, and to enable them to be present at the same.

Second. Because said notices do contain statements of the facts to be proven by this Contestant, together with a list of the witnesses by whom the same were to be so proven, and that the said notices and the said testimony, in every particular of form and substance, are in strict and literal conformity with the requirements of the Code, Section 32, of the Acts of 1865, chapter 143, in regard to contested elections, and that the said forms of notice adopted by this Contestant have been fully recognized by your Honorable predecessors in the contested election case from Allegany County, 1867 (as per House Document O of that body), as ample, sufficient and legal, and the same have been further adopted by the said Robert S. Widdicombe, and that he is now engaged in taking proof in support of his own claim or pretentions to said office, under notices served upon this respondent, similar in every respect of form and substance with those objected to.

Wherefore, this Contestant prays that said objections may be dismissed and as in duty bound.

HENRY BROOKE,

Contestant, P. P.

Filed with me this 26th day of January, 1874.

[SEAL.]　　　　　　　　　　　JAMES HARRIS,

Justice of the Peace.